AN INTRODUCTION
TO THE ARCHITECTURAL
HERITAGE *of*

LIMERICK CITY

THOMOND BRIDGE

A view of Thomond Bridge looking towards the recently restored King John's Castle.

Foreword

Limerick is a city that has been in existence for eleven centuries. Shaped by many people and institutions and by its varied roles, it has a rich architectural heritage. A walled medieval city that survived on trade, it retains its frequently attacked and successively fortified castle, some of its walls, part of its Exchange and the tower house of one of its most prominent merchant families. Its crowning glory is St Mary's Cathedral, the only medieval building in the city still in active use. Continuity is also ensured with replacements: two medieval bridges and churches and a market were rebuilt in the early nineteenth century.

As trade flourished in the late eighteenth and early nineteenth centuries Limerick's merchants and patrons became prosperous and ambitious. The result was Newtown Pery, a gridded suburb that contains the largest area of Georgian buildings in Ireland outside Dublin and which forms the commercial core of the city. Here are streets of four-storey brick terraces, corn stores and granaries, public spaces, and the new building types of the period – nonconformist churches, banks and lecture halls. Just beyond the grid are Limerick's versions of the institutional buildings that would appear all over Ireland – the asylum, the gaol, the workhouse and barracks – many still in the use as originally intended.

SARSFIELD BRIDGE

A view down river looking towards Sarsfield Bridge taken when Clancy's Strand (to the right) was a quiet suburb in County Clare.

Courtesy of the National Library of Ireland.

KING'S ISLAND

A contemporary view up river towards King's Island with Sarsfield Bridge in the centre and new riverside buildings to the right.

By the late nineteenth century the river at Limerick was lined with industrial buildings. The mid-nineteenth-century port, a flax spinning factory, parts of the gas works and the Bannatyne Mill all survive. Limerick became part of the railway network, obtained a Model School and a multitude of Victorian civic and commercial structures. Churches, charity institutions, statues, schools and department stores punctuated the new town grid, while suburban houses and convents were built on new arterial roads. Edwardian decorativeness and modern brutalism have added their note to the stock of civic, institutional, residential, commercial and ecclesiastical buildings in the city.

The NIAH survey, which identifies and highlights a representative selection of the architectural heritage of Limerick City, was carried out in the summer and autumn of 2005. It covered 736 buildings, of which 732 have been recommended for protection. The survey is part of a systematic programme of county and city surveys carried out by the Department of the Environment, Heritage and Local Government.

The survey and this Introduction aim to draw attention to the great variety of the built heritage. The larger, impressive buildings such as the cathedrals, Custom House and the few architect-designed Georgian terraces, are readily appreciated for their architectural and historical value. But many of the more modest structures – utilitarian bridges, mills and barracks; buildings that make an impact as a group such as the brick terraces; the smaller, quirkier buildings such as club houses and tollhouses; and features such as shopfronts, railings and bootscrapers – can be overlooked and potentially lost without record. All of these buildings and structures are integral to the experience and architectural character of the city.

The NIAH survey of the architectural heritage of Limerick City can be accessed on the Internet at: *www.buildingsofireland.ie*

NATIONAL INVENTORY *of* ARCHITECTURAL HERITAGE

Foundation of the City to 1691

The first settlement was built on an island (Inis Sibtonn, now King's Island) in a loop of the River Shannon, 90 kilometres from the sea. Just below a rocky outcrop to the south-west of the island was a protected inlet. At the north-west the island was connected by a ford to Thomond (now County Clare) and at the south there was another ford. It was an ideal place to settle, well-defended, with a natural harbour and access to the surrounding lands.

By the early tenth century the Vikings established a stronghold at this location from which they conducted raids along the length of the River Shannon. In 969 the Dál gCais from Thomond took control, and the resulting Hiberno-Norse walled town, centred on the harbour, flourished for the next 230 years *(fig. 1)*. It is possible that the church of St Mary, which existed when Limerick was declared a diocese at the Synod of Ráth Breasail in 1111, stood on the present site of the cathedral above the harbour. The Anglo-Normans took over for a brief period in the 1170s when they built a ringwork fort outside the walls close to the Thomond ford. After they had gone circular dwellings were built just south of its ditch.

(fig. 1)
DRAUGHT OF THE
COUNTRY ROUND
LIMERICK
c.1752

This map, drawn by William Eyres, illustrates Limerick and its environs in c.1752 in the aftermath of the sieges. The original settlement was at the south-west of the island. The roads to Dublin, Cork, Ennis and Adare are clearly shown. Thomond Bridge, connecting Englishtown to County Clare, was built above Curragour Falls.

Courtesy of the British Library.

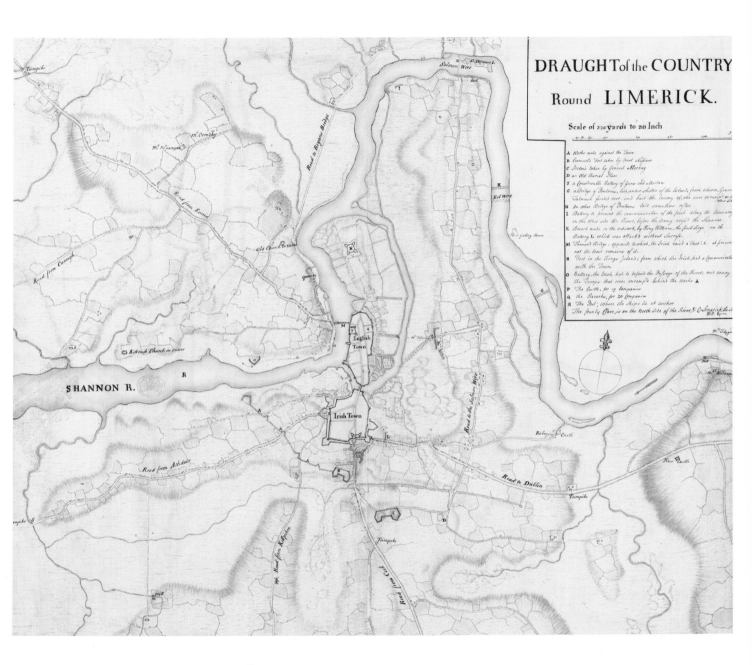

DRAUGHT of the COUNTRY
Round LIMERICK.

Scale of 320 yards to an Inch

A Works made against the Town
B Cromwels Fort taken by Count Nassaw
C Ireton's taken by General Mackay
D an Old Burial Place
E a Considerable Battery of Guns and Mortars
G a Bridge of Pontoons, laid under shelter of the Islands, from whence, Genera...
   Talmach forded over, and had the Enemy of, who were encamp'd on...
H An other Bridge of Pontoons, laid sometime after.
I Battery to prevent the communication of the Irish along the Shore ever...
   on the other side the River, before the Army crossed the Shannon.
K Breach made in the outwork, by King William, the first Siege on the
   Battery L. which was attack'd without Success.
M Thomond Bridge, opposite to which, the Irish raised a Fort: b. at presen...
   not the least remains of it.
N Fort in the Kings Island; from which the Irish had a Communicatio...
   with the Town.
O Battery, the Irish had to defend the Passage of the River, and among...
   the Troops that were encamp'd behind the Works A.
P The Castle, for 12 Companies
Q the Barracks, for 20 Companies
R The Pool, where the Ships lie at anchor
   The County Clare, is on the North side of the River, & of Limerick the...
   William Byrne.

SHANNON R.

English Town

Irish Town

(fig. 2)
KING JOHN'S CASTLE
Thirteenth century

A view of the D-shaped gatehouse towers (1211-12) with the later north-west tower in the background. A royal castle with curtain walls and corner towers, it provided a modestly provisioned and protected area for the constable and garrison.

(fig. 3)
KING JOHN'S CASTLE
Thirteenth century

Recent excavation has
revealed the late thirteenth-
century hall built along the
western curtain wall. Four
loops (they are segmental-
headed openings on the
inside) lit the lower level.

The Anglo-Normans took possession of
Limerick again in 1195 after the death of
Domhnall Mór Ua Briain. The city became a royal borough, and John, Lord of Ireland (later King
John) granted it a charter in 1197 in which the
citizens were given modest self-government and
the right to pursue business interests without
undue interference. The Crown strengthened the
defences of the city, an undertaking that was
stretched over 300 years. Work started at King
John's Castle in the first decade of the thirteenth
century. Initially an enlarging of the extramural
twelfth-century ringwork, it was soon absorbed
into the city walls. Large circular limestone towers were built to the north-east and north-west
and were joined by a curtain wall punctuated by
two gatehouse towers *(figs. 2-3)*. Later, a curtain
wall was built to a south-west tower. There was
no south-east tower.

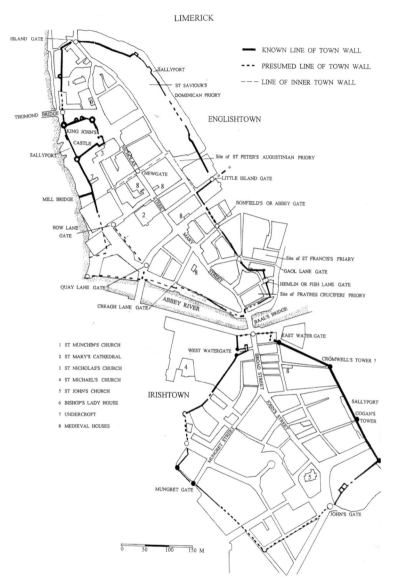

LIMERICK

KNOWN LINE OF TOWN WALL

PRESUMED LINE OF TOWN WALL

LINE OF INNER TOWN WALL

ISLAND GATE

SALLYPORT

ST SAVIOUR'S
DOMINICAN PRIORY

ENGLISHTOWN

THOMOND BRIDGE

KING JOHN'S
CASTLE

SALLYPORT

Site of ST PETER'S AUGUSTINIAN PRIORY

NEWGATE

LITTLE ISLAND GATE

BONFIELD'S OR ABBEY GATE

MILL BRIDGE

BOW LANE
GATE

Site of ST FRANCIS'S FRIARY

GAOL LANE GATE

HEMLIN OR FISH LANE GATE

Site of FRATRES CRUCIFERI PRIORY

QUAY LANE GATE

CREAGH LANE GATE

ABBEY RIVER

BAAL'S BRIDGE

EAST WATER GATE

WEST WATERGATE

CROMWELL'S TOWER ?

IRISHTOWN

SALLYPORT

COGAN'S
TOWER

1 ST MUNCHIN'S CHURCH

2 ST MARY'S CATHEDRAL

3 ST NICHOLAS'S CHURCH

4 ST MICHAEL'S CHURCH

5 ST JOHN'S CHURCH

6 BISHOP'S LADY HOUSE

7 UNDERCROFT

8 MEDIEVAL HOUSES

MUNGRET GATE

JOHN'S GATE

0   50   100   150 M

(fig. 4)
MAP OF THE CITY WALL

A map of the walls based on recent archaeological work and superimposed on a recent street plan. The original was drawn by Claire Lane in 1988 and updated by Celie ORahilly as investigation revealed more of the wall up to 2001.

Courtesy of Celie ORahilly.

With the murage grants of 1237 and 1311, the walled town to the south of the castle was extended to enclose the northern suburb, the whole becoming known as Englishtown. The southern suburb, known as Irishtown, which had grown up on the far side of the Abbey River within the parish of St John, was walled mainly during the fifteenth century. The high walls, battlemented by the seventeenth century, were punctuated by towers and gates *(figs. 4-6)*. Portions of the wall, built in uncoursed rubble limestone quarried locally, survives, though it is not always obvious, for the remains are

(fig. 6)
LIMERICK CITY
1611

John Speed's map of Limerick, published in 1611, is broadly accurate in its depiction of the two walled towns with the main street running through, connected by Baal's Bridge. Inaccurate is the river flowing directly below all the walls and the spire on St Mary's Cathedral.

Courtesy of Limerick City Museum.

(fig. 5)
LIMERICK CITY
c.1590

This map of the city dates to c.1590. The walls and street pattern of Englishtown and Irishtown are clearly identifiable as are surviving buildings such as King John's Castle and St Mary's Cathedral.

Courtesy of Trinity College Dublin.

(fig. 7)
JOHN'S GATE
Grounds of
St John's Hospital
Late medieval

John's Gate is a late
medieval structure which
was adapted to form part
of the citadel in 1652-53.
It has a portcullis groove,
pronounced batter and is
constructed of relatively
small squared coarsely
tooled limestone.

fragmentary and many are covered in vegeta-
tion or hidden by buildings. There are large
stretches at the south-east corner of Irishtown
and to the east of Englishtown. John's Gate, a
late medieval rectangular structure with pointed arched openings, situated in the remains of
the southern wall of Irishtown, still stands *(fig.
7)*. Towers too survive. One, circular, sits near a
stretch of now unbattlemented wall behind St
Munchin's Church north of the castle.

The town that grew and prospered both within and without these walls was a port, whose leading citizens were merchants exporting agricultural produce such as corn, rape, hides and salmon, and importing, among other things, wine, iron and salt. Construction on St Mary's Cathedral started in either the late twelfth century (possibly under the patronage of Domhnall Mór Ua Briain) or in the early thirteenth century (possibly replacing the earlier church). Externally its original outline has been lost with the addition of later medieval side chapels *(fig. 8)*. Inside, however, the large square piers with their elongated scallop-decorated sandstone capitals supporting austerely undecorated pointed arches, and the round-headed clerestory windows of the original nave with its narrow side aisles define the heart of a building designed under the influence of the Cistercians *(fig. 15)*. The fine Romanesque west door, made of sandstone with foliate capitals, was possibly taken from the earlier church. It was heavily restored in the nineteenth century. Facing the river, this doorway was the main entrance until the seventeenth century.

The progressive enlarging of the cathedral occurred in the next 300 years: north and south transepts were built in the thirteenth century; the north and south walls were arched and chapels were added in the fourteenth and fifteenth centuries. These were paid for by the wealthy merchant families of the city who also donated tombs and furnishings. Prominent amongst the survivals is the early fifteenth-century Galwey-Bultingfort monument, which is set into the south wall of the south transept and has an intricately carved hood and finial *(fig. 9)*. The beautiful late fifteenth-century oak misericords (seats for clerics), unique in Ireland,

are decorated with both fantastical and real animals and figures in a lively and realistic style *(figs. 10-13)*. Situated above St George's Chapel, at the south-west corner of the church, with narrow round-headed windows set in pairs, is the only medieval domestic-scaled room still in existence in Limerick.

O'BRIEN MONUMENT
St Mary's Cathedral
Nicholas Street
Renewed 1678

This monument is situated
in the chancel of the
Cathedral. The lower
effigy represents Donough
O'Brien, Earl of Thomond
who died 1624. The upper
effigy represents his count-
ess, Lady Elizabeth
Fitzgerald.

(fig. 9)
**GALWEY-BULTINGFORT
MONUMENT**
St Mary's Cathedral
Nicholas Street
South Transept
1414

The monument commemo-
rates Richard Bultingfort
and Geoffry Galwey who
both died in 1414.

(figs. 10-13)
ST MARY'S CATHEDRAL
Nicholas Street
c.1480-1500

There are 23 stalls.
Illustrated clockwise from
top left: a lion in conflict
with a wyvern (a heraldic
beast); an antelope with
serrated horns; a wyvern
biting its tail; a human
head in a chaperon (form
of hat).

(fig. 14)
ST MARY'S CATHEDRAL
Nicholas Street

Interior photograph facing west, which dates to 1880, showing William Slater's seating of 1858-61 which occupied two thirds of the nave.

Courtesy of the National Library of Ireland.

Today the cathedral's interior and exterior are strongly marked by the mid-nineteenth-century restorations of William Slater and George Edmund Street *(figs. 14-15)*. Under the influence of the Ecclesiological movement, they aimed to return the church to a hypothetical late thirteenth-century ideal. Slater, for example, replaced a recently built Perpendicular style east window with a triple lancet. There are also subtly eye-catching early twentieth-century additions; the reredos (1907) and limestone screen (1922) designed by Conor O'Brien, the bronze chancel gates of 1929 and the stained glass in the north transept. They all exhibit the high quality prized by the Arts and Crafts movement. The late twentieth-century restoration has endowed the church with beautiful stone floors.

The basic medieval street pattern, dominated by a main road that runs from Thomond Bridge in Englishtown, over Baal's Bridge and bifurcates in Irishtown, remains. So too do the side streets and lanes that join the spine road and originally divided the burgage plots. The main road linked Limerick to Dublin, Cork and Galway. Medieval Thomond Bridge and Baal's Bridge, which had replaced the earlier fords, were themselves replaced in the mid-nineteenth century.

(fig. 15)
ST MARY'S CATHEDRAL
Nicholas Street

Interior view facing east towards the twentieth-century limestone screen and reredos, which shows the arcade and clerestory of the original church and the barrel vault erected by William Slater in 1858-61. The triple lancet east window has stained glass by Clayton & Bell commissioned in 1859.

There are no remains of the timber cagework houses that would have characterized the medieval town, but by the late sixteenth century part of the main street in Englishtown and Irishtown were lined with four- and five-storey battlemented stone houses with gables facing the street. Some of these, including one said to be the residence of the former mayor, Dominick Fanning, were conceived as tower houses *(fig. 16)*. This building has four storeys, one room per floor, over a vaulted undercroft. Its large chamfered limestone openings are typical of late medieval work in the region. A smaller house on Curry's Lane in Irishtown has similar details *(fig. 17)*. Two fragments of medieval industry remain. Part of the walls and the housing for the wheel axle of King's Mills can be seen in the river wall just beyond the cathedral. A bridge with pointed arches that once connected the mill to the shore is buried under the river terrace. A weir of possibly Viking origin (known as Laxweir), but mostly rebuilt, stands at the far north of the island *(fig. 18)*. The east side of Englishtown was lined with religious foundations some of which were incorporated into the walled area. All that remains of these is the north wall of the church and the east wall of the Dominican Friary, founded in 1227 *(fig. 19)*.

(fig. 16)
FANNING'S CASTLE
Mary Street
Sixteenth century

The pairs of ogee windows on the second and third floors imply a certain level of luxury for the sixteenth-century inhabitants.

(fig. 17)
CURRY'S LANE

Detail of the very badly neglected remains of a row of medieval houses. A late medieval window opening with limestone surrounds and relieving arch and a pointed head doorway are visible on left of the picture.

(fig. 18)
LAXWEIR

This view of the laxweir ('lax' meaning salmon) looks towards a medieval castle, Caslaunnacorran, situated on St Thomas island. The piers of the weir are twentieth century.

Courtesy of Limerick City Museum.

(fig. 19)
TOWN WALL
Englishtown

This photograph, which dates from 1890-1915, shows a view of the surviving town wall at the north-east side of Englishtown adjacent to the thirteenth-century Dominican Friary. It has two blocked arched openings that may have given the friars access to the extramural fields and orchards to the east shown on the c.1590 map of the city.

Courtesy of Limerick City Museum.

With the Reformation and the Tudor effort to re-assert control in Ireland, Limerick was brought more closely into national affairs in the sixteenth century. One still visible manifestation of this was the building of the bastion - the south face and western flank of the present structure are original - at the south-east corner of the castle in 1611 *(fig. 20)*. The seventeenth century proved to be exceptionally bloody in Limerick. The Confederate siege of the castle in 1642 left an intriguing legacy of mines and countermines, recently unearthed during archaeological investigations. Cromwell's forces took Limerick after a long siege in the summer of 1651 and secured their presence by constructing a citadel with two bastions facing the city at John's Gate in Irishtown in 1652-3 *(fig. 21)*.

The late seventeenth century saw a flowering of civic activity and pride. Gates were rebuilt and given Latin inscriptions. A County Courthouse, a new Exchange and City Courthouse were built, the latter two situated near St Mary's Cathedral, defining that area as the centre of the city. Only the Exchange, as rebuilt in the eighteenth century, partially survives. Preparations for the final act in the war between William of Orange and the Jacobites in 1691 erased much, particularly the suburbs outside the walls. But they left numerous maps showing Englishtown and Irishtown walls underscored by extensive extramural fortifications only linked by the gated Baal's Bridge. They described a well-defended and an apparently divided city *(fig. 22)*.

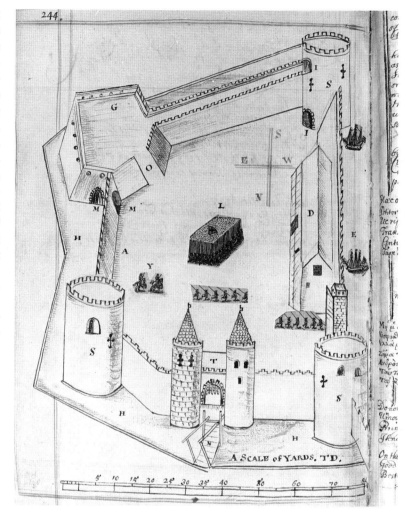

(fig. 20)
**KING JOHN'S CASTLE
1611**

This drawing of King John's Castle is part of Thomas Dineley's *Tour of Ireland* describing his journey of 1680. The bastion (top left hand corner), constructed in the aftermath of the Nine Years War by Josiah Bodley, was part of his work strengthening the fortifications in Ireland against not only external attack but internal revolt.

Courtesy of the Photographic Unit, Department of the Environment, Heritage and Local Government.

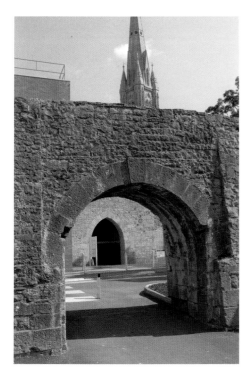

(fig. 21)
ENTRANCE TO CITADEL
Grounds of
St John's Hospital
1652-53

This view shows the round-arched entrance of the Cromwellian citadel, with its projecting keystone, through which the guard-house, the converted medieval gate, can be seen.

(fig. 22)
LIMERICK CITY
Eighteenth century

An eighteenth-century French map of Limerick showing the medieval walls, and the extramural fortifications constructed in 1690 and 1691. Most attention was paid to Irishtown where four bastions and a demi-lune were built to project from the walls, beyond which was a ditch and a covered way surrounded by a timber palisade. The walls themselves were 25-30 feet high (7.6 x 9.1m), four-five feet thick (1.2 x 1.5m) and had a three-foot (0.9m) walkway on top.

Courtesy of Limerick City Museum.

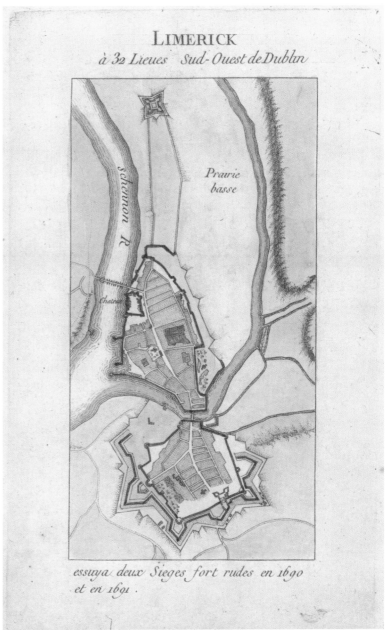

LIMERICK
à 32 Lieues Sud-Ouest de Dublin

essuya deux Sieges fort rudes en 1690 et en 1691.

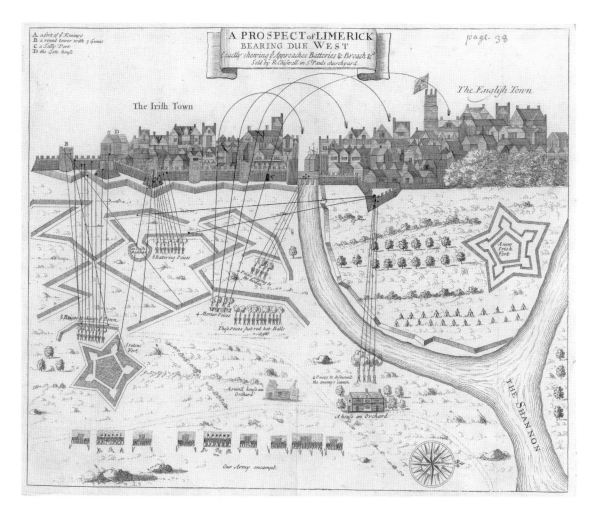

**LIMERICK CITY
1693**

This illustration is titled 'A Prospect of Limerick Bearing Due West, Exactly Shewing the Batteries Approaches & Breach etc.' and was published in *A True and Impartial History of the Most Material Occurrences in the Kingdom of Ireland During the Two Last Years With the Present State of Both Armies* by George Story (1693). It depicts the Williamites' attack on the east side of Limerick in 1690. The book was written by an eye witness.

Courtesy of the Leonard Collection, University of Limerick.

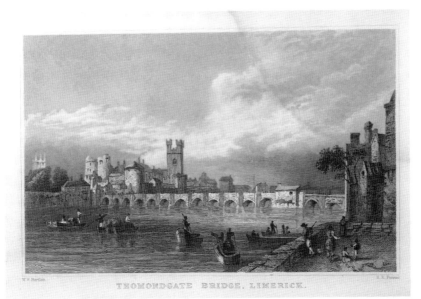

THOMONDGATE BRIDGE, LIMERICK.

THOMOND BRIDGE

This view, by William Henry Bartlett (1809-1854), shows the medieval bridge with the old toll-house between the third and fourth pier to the right, the castle in ruins and St Mary's Cathedral behind. It became a classic view of Limerick.

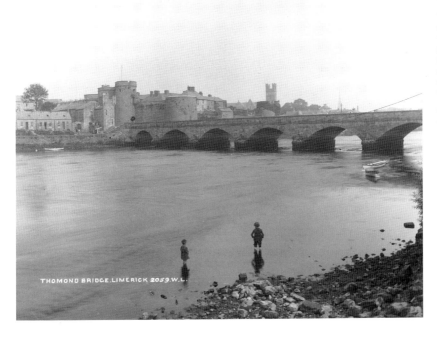

THOMOND BRIDGE, LIMERICK 2059.W.L.

THOMOND BRIDGE

This Lawrence Collection photograph shows the 1840 Thomond Bridge designed by James and George Pain with the tollhouse on the left. The castle survives as the most conspicuous element of the medieval fortifications.

Courtesy of the National Library of Ireland.

21

1691-c.1790

Recovery from the destruction and loss of morale caused by the siege of 1691 was slow. A catastrophic explosion in a harbour battery in 1693 was a further set back, and the economy did not begin to grow significantly until the late 1740s. The Williamite victory in 1691 decisively strengthened British control in Ireland, and the subsequent penal laws ensured Protestant ascendancy and severe economic and ideological disadvantage for Catholics. This underscored the balance of power established in the late seventeenth century when Protestants had gained the upper hand in the city's Corporation under the government regulations of 1672. Furthermore, an influx of Dutch weavers and merchants and English settlers, together with Catholics who had converted, all of whom had benefited from the Cromwellian resettlement, meant that much land within the walls was in Protestant hands. Under the Penal Laws old Catholic merchant families such as the Creaghs, Roches, and Arthurs were liable to quarterage fees if they lived within the Corporation's jurisdiction, and they were excluded from office. Of the four Catholic chapels built between 1730 and 1781, only one, the Dominican chapel near Baal's Bridge, was situated within the city walls *(fig. 23)*. It also happened to be the smallest, earliest and the only one of which a remnant - the east wall - survives.

Until the walls were officially declared redundant in 1760 most building work was carried out within the medieval town and, due to the perceived Jacobite threat, attention was still paid to the city's fortifications. Surviving nineteenth-century photographs testify to the extensive reconstruction of the existing stone terraced houses facing the main streets of Englishtown and Irishtown. They were given high brick facades with regularly placed vertical sash windows and curved or triangular pediments in a style that derived from seventeenth-century Dutch domestic architecture *(figs. 24-25)*. Unfortunately, the only survivals are a pair of brick Dutch gables at the rear of John's Square, and a single gable on Broad Street. The recently renovated Bishop's Palace near the castle is a medieval stone house reworked in the early eighteenth century, though without a new brick façade *(fig. 26)*.

A pioneering domestic development just inside the walls at John's Gate struck a new note. It was the inspiration of the young Edmund Sexton Pery, an aspiring politician who would later become Speaker of the Irish parliament. The heir of the wealthy Limerick family, the Sextons, he inherited vast tracts of land both within and without the walls. John's Square was a speculative venture, aiming to attract wealthy families with country seats to winter in the city as their counterparts were

(fig. 24)
MARY STREET

The photograph of these Dutch-gabled houses on Mary Street was taken sometime between 1890 and 1915 when they had become tenements.

Courtesy of Limerick City Museum.

(fig. 23)
DOMINICAN CHAPEL
Fish Lane
1780

This photograph was taken just prior to its demolition and shows that the Dominican chapel was a galleried structure. A drawing of the front façade reveals that it was a converted four-bay three-storey house with round-headed windows on the first floor. Only the brick built east wall of the chapel survives.

Courtesy of Limerick City Museum.

(fig. 25)
BROAD STREET

This view shows the backs of four gabled houses on Broad Street. Their early eighteenth-century sash windows were probably inserted into medieval walls.

Courtesy of Limerick City Museum.

(fig. 26)
BISHOP'S PALACE
Church Street
Early eighteenth century

Five bays wide with a Venetian doorway in cut stone, its size and classical detailing echo the modest country houses being built in the early eighteenth century. The building was restored by Limerick Civic Trust in 1990.

(fig. 28)
JOHN'S SQUARE

(fig. 27)
JOHN'S SQUARE
1751-57

Three storeys over vaulted basements with a defined attic storey of smaller square windows, the eight houses in John's Square made a gesture to the Palladian proportioning that was becoming increasingly common in London and Dublin. They were decorated in cut local limestone and brick with oculi, niches and shouldered architraves.

(fig. 29)
JOHN'S SQUARE

doing in Waterford and Dublin. Probably designed by the artist and architect, Francis Bindon, the eight houses formed three sides of a square, with a brick-lined niche and oculus between each pair of houses. Surprisingly, given the vogue for brick, they were built in squared coursed limestone, and had eaves instead of parapets. Two double-sized houses were added later to enlarge the square, which remains an isolated enclave of distinctive character *(figs. 27-29)*.

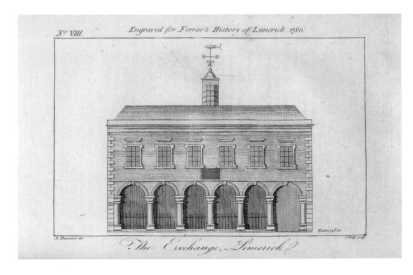

No VIII.   Engraved for Ferrar's History of Limerick, 1786.

A. Dominick del.   Exand by Fecit   J.Roff Sculp

The Exchange, Limerick

The other major development within the medieval city was the rebuilding, in the classical idiom, of public buildings first constructed near St Mary's Cathedral in the mid-seventeenth century. The Exchange, rebuilt in 1778, was a sizeable and relatively elegant version of the open ground floor market/first floor town hall combination common in Ireland from the mid-eighteenth century. It had limestone quoins, Tuscan columns, shouldered architraves and a lantern *(fig. 30)*. Another modestly classical limestone building, the City Courthouse, situated round the corner on Quay Lane (now Bridge Street), has fared better and is now a school *(fig. 31)*. The Blue Coat School of 1772, which still stands, was initiated by the cathedral dean, Charles Massy. It is a plain building tucked against the side of the cathedral and partially hidden behind a high wall. Its windows have pointed heads, an early example of scholastic Gothic *(fig. 32)*.

(fig. 30)
THE EXCHANGE
Nicholas Street
1778

Today only the Tuscan columns survive as part of St Mary's graveyard wall.

Courtesy of the Leonard Collection, University of Limerick.

(fig. 31)
GAELSCOIL
(former City Courthouse)
Bridge Street
1763-65, remodelled 1845

The courthouse has a breakfront and pediment, cut stone architraves, sills and quoins and a separate gateway. It was remodelled in 1845 when it became a school.

(fig. 32)
BLUE COAT SCHOOL
Nicholas Street
1772

The old school building is the gabled structure with the pointed arch windows situated between the east wall of the cathedral and the flat-roofed house.

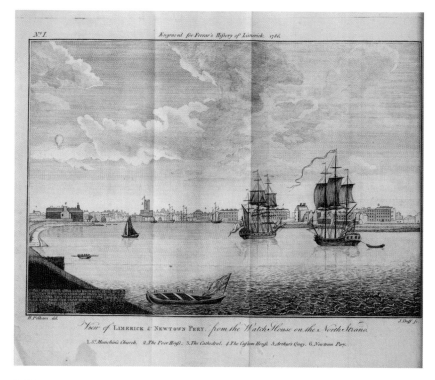

VIEW OF LIMERICK AND NEWTOWN PERY

This view, from the 1787 edition of John Ferrar's, *The History of Limerick*, shows Englishtown (at the centre left) to the Bishop's Palace (at the right). With the building of a Custom House and new quays on the Shannon, and a concentration of new buildings – Arthur's Quay terrace (centre), the House of Industry (to the far left) and the Bishop's Palace – on the river front, Limerick had the appearance of a significantly expanded port by 1787.

Courtesy of the Leonard Collection, University of Limerick.

VIEW OF LIMERICK

A late nineteenth-century photograph depicting the same view of riverside Limerick from Englishtown to the Bishop's Palace. By the mid-nineteenth century Limerick was consolidated as an expanded port whose quays were lined with mills and warehouses. It had a new bridge, Wellesley Bridge (far left), linking the city to County Clare.

Courtesy of the National Library of Ireland.

A VIEW OF LIMERICK
c.1820

This view, by William
Turner de Lond, shows
the Abbey River looking
towards the old Mathew
Bridge with the medieval
Englishtown behind
George's Quay to the
right, Bank Place in the left
foreground and the new
County Courthouse promi-
nent in the background.

*Courtesy of the Knight
of Glin.*

(fig. 33)
BANK PLACE
c.1790

The buildings display more crafted stonework than later terraced houses. Today a pedimented stone doorcase, shouldered architraves, stone keystones to the windows and moulded sills survive.

Courtesy of Limerick City Museum.

From the early eighteenth century entrepreneurs had been looking at building quays along the Abbey River as an alternative to the confined medieval port and as a way of sidestepping heavy tolls imposed by the Corporation which was ruled by a corrupt oligarchy. But it was not until Edmund Sexton Pery (MP for Limerick in 1760) petitioned for government grants, available because of plans to make the Shannon navigable from Limerick to Leitrim, that large-scale work began. By the early 1760s, with the medieval town wall bordering the Abbey River demolished, a new quay stretched along the north bank of the Abbey River from the battery at the tip of the old port almost to Baal's Bridge. Part of a canal had been dug near Lock Quay and there were plans for more quays, all of which were built subsequently. A new bridge, the steeply rising predecessor of the 1846 Mathew Bridge, linked medieval Bridge Street on the island to this development. Independent initiatives were encouraged by an act of 1759, which provided incentives for capital expenditure on land adjoining cities. This was particularly attractive to Catholics and those outside the Corporation oligarchy who paid high taxes and reaped few benefits.

In 1764 Andrew Welsh opened Lock Mills, a water-operated flour mill at the entrance to the canal, of which the inscribed cut stone entrance remains *(fig. 41)*. Urban development soon followed, with four-storey brick terraces with Palladian parapets, proportioning and the pedimented doorcases popular in Dublin appearing on the new quays - Charlotte Quay, George's Quay and Bank Place. Three houses on Bank Place remain *(figs. 33-34)*. In 1770, three years before that of Waterford, a classicised Assembly House was opened on what became Assembly Mall. It was demolished in 1838 *(fig. 35)*.

(fig. 34)
BANK PLACE

Detail of doorcase architrave.

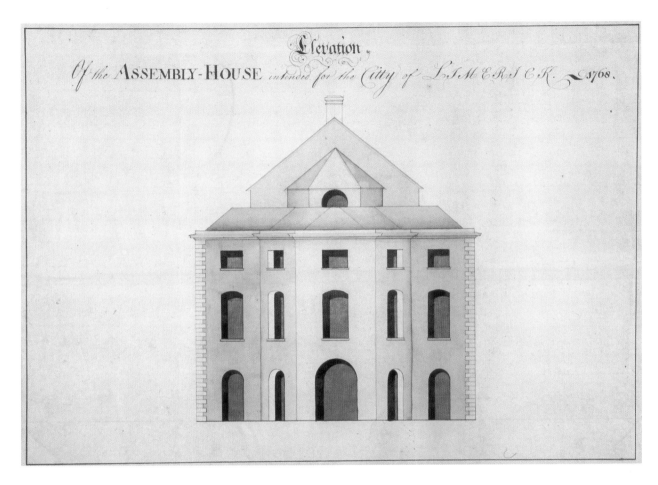

Elevation
Of the ASSEMBLY-HOUSE *intended for the City of* LIMERICK *1768.*

(fig. 35)
**ELEVATION OF THE
ASSEMBLY-HOUSE
INTENDED FOR THE
CITY OF LIMERICK
1768**

The Assembly House was a three-storey building with a central three-sided bay and octagon. It contained one of the first purpose-built ballrooms in Ireland. The drawing is unsigned and may not be by the architect of the building, the Reverend Deane Hoare.

Courtesy of the Knight of Glin.

ELEVATION of the Front of the Custom-House now building in LIMERICK (MDCCLXVI) Extent 175 FEET

(fig. 36)
CUSTOM HOUSE
Rutland Street
1765-69

This drawing was published in the first edition of John Ferrar's, *An History of the City of Limerick* (1767) and shows Davis Dukart's proposed design. The inscription on the breakfront and chamfers to the wing pier panels were omitted in the final building. It is now the Hunt Museum.

Courtesy of the Leonard Collection, University of Limerick.

CUSTOM HOUSE
c.1844

A well-travelled topographical artist William Henry Bartlett (1809-1854) has here shown the Custom House as the busy heart of the city with its crane, adjacent warehouses, and the activity associated with arriving and departing boats. He has included estuary tenders and British trading vessels, all were probably added in his studio.

CUSTOM HOUSE, LIMERICK.

(fig. 37)
HUNT MUSEUM
(former Custom House)
Rutland Street

Detail of pilaster capital.

(fig. 38)
HUNT MUSEUM
(former Custom House)
Rutland Street

This view of the rusticated base and first floor window shows that Davis Dukart's detailing was superbly executed on the riverfront in Kilkenny limestone.

Pivotal to this newly ambitious commercial expansion with its up-to-date domestic architecture was the Custom House. It was built between 1765 and 1769 beside a partially finished quay on the River Shannon just south of the New Bridge. It was situated opposite the old port and at the head of a new road, which ran south away from the old centre. Efficiently prodded by Edmund Sexton Pery, the Revenue Commissioners employed the newly arrived Italian architect/engineer of conservative taste and great appetite for work, Davis Dukart, instead of the previously commissioned local architect, Edward Smyth. Dukart's fine piece of architecture to be executed in stone was to be considerably more expensive than Smyth's brick building; at over £10,000, much more than the Commissioners had anticipated. Dukart produced a graceful Palladian-inspired design of central block and single-storey wings, which combined practicality with a leisurely air, and gave Limerick a handsome building of substantial architectural merit *(fig. 36)*. Dukart, an eclectic, brought a variety of influences to his details, such as vermiculated keystones, a rusticated base, roundels and a breakfront, the latter decorated with finely fluted pilasters and Composite capitals *(figs. 37-38)*. Inside there was a long room – the public desk – and on the top floor an apartment for the collector and his family.

(fig. 40)
THE GRANARY
Bank Place
1787

(fig. 39)
4 PATRICK STREET
c.1780

At about the same time and continuing into the next decade, the area between the Custom House and the western walls of the Irishtown, was speculatively developed by Limerick merchants. Foremost among these was the Catholic timber merchant, Patrick Arthur and his son, Francis, who built brick terraces on Arthur's Quay facing the Shannon, on Patrick Street (a continuation of the new road), and on Francis Street, all similar to the earlier terrace on Bank Place. Number 4 Patrick Street (the house in which the opera singer, Catherine Hayes was born) survives largely intact *(fig. 39)*. The

mouldings and profiles of its interior joinery – stairs, panelled doors, shutters and skirtings – set a pattern that would be followed for the next seventy years. Meanwhile other merchants, including the Catholic, Philip Roche, were setting a precedent with the construction of warehouses, many for corn and wheat, outside the Irishtown walls. Several still survive, most notably the five-storey granary, renovated in the 1970s *(fig. 40)*. They are a variation on the multi-storey Lock Mills: five- and six-storey buildings (floors known as lofts) in random rubble limestone with small arched windows formed in brick, and a strip of timber loading doors with a projecting overhead sack hoist on the gable *(fig. 41)*.

(fig. 41)
LOCK MILLS
1764

The mill was built for Andrew Welsh by Edward Uzuld, a prominent Limerick builder, in 1762-4 at a cost of £6,000. It had six pairs of mill stones for corn, four bolting mills and four tucking mills. It had the first machine in Ireland for separating bran from flour and each quality of flour from the other. Water was supplied to the mill from the canal, for which the Shannon Navigation was paid £40 per annum.

Courtesy of Limerick City Museum.

Newtown Pery
1765-c.1840

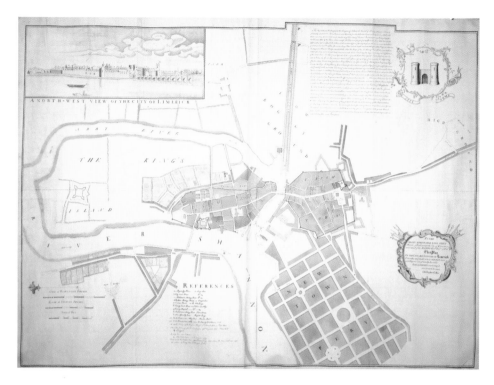

(fig. 43)
**PERY SQUARE TO
KING'S ISLAND**

A mid-twentieth-century
aerial view from Pery
Square to King's Island
with Catherine Street in
the centre. Much remains,
though some buildings
have gone, most noticeably
Arthur's Quay and Francis
Place terraces and stores.

*Courtesy of English
Heritage.*

(fig. 42)
**LIMERICK CITY AND
SUBURBS
1769**

Christopher Colles's map
of the city, which dates to
1769, includes a survey
of the existing city and a
proposal for Newtown Pery
designed by Davis Dukart.
This quarter was an irregular open grid centred on
a main street linking it to
Englishtown, enlivened by
a variety of suggested
squares.

*Courtesy of the British
Library.*

In 1765, at the time of the Custom House commission, Edmund Sexton Pery had paid Davis Dukart to design a town plan for the land he owned to the south of the city, known as South Prior's Land. Dukart produced a grid of streets interspersed with three squares *(fig. 42)*. It was bounded on the west by the Shannon, on the north by the new development and on the east by the existing Boherbuoy Road. It roughly doubled the size of the city. Plots were leased and sub-leased largely by merchants, builders and lawyers, and were gradually built on in the next 75 years. The leases specified that the roads should be 60 feet wide (18.29m), and that a rear stable lane, 12 or 15 feet wide (3.66-4.57m), should service each block. Leaseholders of plots next to the river were permitted to construct quays of a maximum 60 feet wide (18.29m). There was an attempt to realise one of the squares with a chapel of ease at the centre, but this was later abandoned. The two public spaces that now exist – the Crescent and Pery Square – were not to the exact design or in the exact location of the master plan; they resulted from the initiatives of the men who leased the adjacent plots.

With the economy still sluggish development was initially slow. The first plots were sold in the 1770s. They were mainly on land adjacent to the Irishtown walls, the Shannon and the Boherbuoy Road, with a few isolated plots on the main grid. Sales of leases increased when the economy revived, especially with the outbreak of the Napoleonic Wars in 1803 and the growth in the provisions trade. Many plots on the main axis, George's Street (now O'Connell Street), the parallel street, Catherine Street and on the crossing streets were sold in the early 1800s *(figs. 43-44)*. By 1815 most of the present streets had some buildings on them. The next 20 years was a period of consolidation. In the late 1830s a few new streets, including Pery Square, were built at the southern (upper end) of the new town.

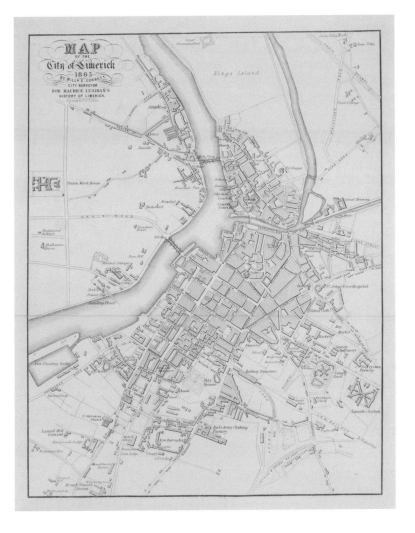

(fig. 44)
MAP OF THE CITY OF LIMERICK 1865

This map of the city by William Edward Corbett, City Surveyor, for Maurice Lenihan's *History of Limerick* (1866), shows the grid as it had been realised in the mid-nineteenth century.

Courtesy of Trinity College Dublin.

Although a number of the buildings have been subsequently replaced and many have been altered (though not irrevocably), Newtown Pery is still a recognisable and impressive Georgian new town. Contemporary visitors were frequently admiring: they found it flourishing, the streets were wide and modern looking, the buildings elegant. The main streets were lined with four-storey over basement brick terraces. They had parapets, sash windows of the adapted Palladian proportions of townhouses in Dublin and London, tooled ashlar stone basements, limestone sills, steps to the front door, iron railings set on limestone

(fig. 46)
68 O'CONNELL STREET
c.1820

The builders in the 1820s, and particularly in the late 1830s in the upper part of the new town, followed Palladian rules more closely by making the first floor piano nobile windows longer (more than a double square) than the ground floor windows. They also tended to add cast-iron balconies of varied designs.

(fig. 45)
GEORGE'S STREET

This photograph shows the lower end of George's Street (now O'Connell Street) where shops occupied most of the ground floors.

Courtesy of the National Library of Ireland.

(fig. 47)
MALLOW STREET
c.1830

Some of the brick for the terraces was made locally; there were brick fields at Coonagh and Singland. The limestone was quarried locally; during the period many limestone quarries were opened up around the city, especially on the north bank of the Shannon and to the south and west of the new town.

(fig. 48)
MEWS BUILDING
Catherine Street

The lower and upper openings were often neatly contained within the same brick arch.

plinths, and elaborately carved doorcases in stone or timber with elliptical fanlights *(figs. 45-47)*. The rear walls were in rubble limestone, and it was usual for the staircase windows to be round headed. There were small gardens or yards to the rear. Beyond, there were stable lanes lined with uncoursed rubble limestone mews buildings with wide brick arched entrances for horses and carriages, and small upper windows for the haylofts, at least one of which was converted into a dovecot *(figs. 48-49)*. There were brick vaults under the pavements, accessible from the basement area, for the storage of coal.

(fig. 49)
DOVECOT
96 O'Connell Street
c.1815-20

Mews building with dovecot to first floor and later opening to ground floor.

Courtesy of the Irish Architectural Archive.

Stone corn stores built of uncoursed rubble limestone with small brick-formed arched windows and timber loading doors, some set in large courtyards, others built adjacent to terraces, were also to be found within the grid. Inside, the open floors were supported by timber posts and beams *(fig. 50)*. Many stores and large mill buildings were concentrated in the area near the river, often facing the river where quays had been constructed. There was another concentration on the eastern edge of the town.

Some of the most individual of the surviving buildings of Newtown Pery date from the late eighteenth century. The Round House, built just outside the Irishtown walls where High Street bifurcates, has a curved brick façade which is visible from some distance *(fig. 51)*. Edmund Sexton Pery's brother, William Cecil, Bishop of Limerick from 1784 to 1794, built a new Bishop's Palace on Henry Street, possibly to designs that Christopher Colles made in 1771 for the previous bishop *(figs. 52-54)*. Sometime after 1787 Edmund's son-in-law, Henry Hartstonge built a house adjacent to it *(figs. 55-56)*. These are among the most impressive townhouses in the city.

(fig. 50)
LIMERICK PRINTMAKERS
Robert Street
c.1770

One of the earliest corn stores built outside the Irishtown walls, close to the Abbey River.

(fig. 51)
ROUND HOUSE
High Street
c.1780

(fig. 53)
FORMER BISHOP'S PALACE
Henry Street

(fig. 54)
FORMER BISHOP'S PALACE
Henry Street

(fig. 52)
FORMER BISHOP'S PALACE
Henry Street
c.1785

Three-storey over basement, this house along with Henry Hartstonge's House, was built on a larger scale than other houses in Newtown Pery. They have elaborately carved stair treads and broken pediments over semi-circular fanlights. Both houses had mews buildings designed as side wings – the one next to the bishop's palace survives – and gardens onto the river.

(fig. 55)
FORMER HENRY HARTSTONGE'S HOUSE
Henry Street
c.1790

In Henry Hartstonge's House, the door had sidelights capped with carved plaques, which were not, unfortunately, put back in during the restoration. The delicately worked cast-iron lamp standards still stand outside the house.

Courtesy of the Irish Architectural Archive.

(fig. 56)
FORMER HENRY HARTSTONGE'S HOUSE
Henry Street

(fig. 57)
**CORNER OF LOWER
HARTSTONGE STREET
AND O'CONNELL STREET**
c.1830

The hierarchy between the
main axis and the crossing
streets is obvious at the
corners where the change
in scale is abrupt. The
building on the corner has
recently been restored.

The terraces erected from the 1800s to the early 1840s have a consistency which gives Newtown Pery its identity. They resemble Dublin terraces in the use of brick, in the plastered reveals to the windows and the predominant austerity of the facades. But the scale is slightly smaller, the details of the doors are different and the stone is local limestone rather than granite. Within the overall homogeneity of Limerick's new town there is great variety. This is partly attributable to an accepted hierarchy in which terraces on the main north-south axis, particularly O'Connell Street, were larger than those on the crossing streets *(fig. 57)*. But each street, or even terrace within the street, has its own character. In some cases this was due to the builder, and in others, to the original leaseholder.

With regard to fenestration the houses generally approximate to the rules of Palladian proportioning in which the first floor windows were larger than the ground floor windows and the second and third floor windows decreased in height progressively. In Hartstonge Street and Thomas Street, the top floor windows are square whereas they are longer in Mallow Street and Glentworth Street. However, the proportions on the façades of Thomas Street, which has wider than normal piers between the buildings (a feature common in the early to mid-eighteenth century), are different from most other terraces. Some houses in the new town display Wyatt windows on the front façade (for example, Numbers 52 and 53 Catherine Street), while most of the rear first- and second-floor windows on O'Connell Street are Wyatt windows. The ground-floor windows on Hartstonge Street have semi-circular heads *(fig. 58)*. Unfortunately the majority of the original sash windows, with their small panes of glass, have been replaced, some in the nineteenth century with plate glass, but many more recently with uPVC frames.

(fig. 58)
HARTSTONGE STREET
c.1830

(figs. 59-63)
DOORCASES
1800-35

Illustrated clockwise from top left: 4 The Crescent, 5 The Crescent, 56 O'Connell Street, 57 O'Connell Street, 8 Mallow Street.

Some houses are two, others three bays wide. The parapet heights are remarkably consistent on O'Connell Street, but highly irregular on Upper Cecil Street. Readily appreciated variety can be seen in the doorcases *(figs. 59-63)*. Sidelights are more usual on O'Connell Street. Fanlights on smaller buildings are flatter and simpler, while on larger buildings the thin metal radiating glazing-bars form elaborate designs suggesting spiders' webs and peacocks' tails *(figs. 64-69)*. There was also great variety in the doorcase details, especially the capitals *(figs. 70-75)*. Cast-iron bootscrapers and pavement covers to the coal openings survive in some places, most notably Pery Square and O'Connell Street *(fig. 76)*.

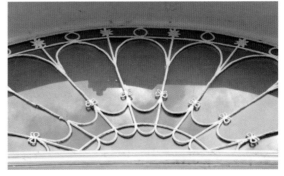

(figs. 64-69)
FANLIGHTS
1800-35

Illustrated clockwise from top left: 4 The Crescent, 1 The Crescent, 56 O'Connell Street, 70 O'Connell Street, 7 The Crescent, 23 Mallow Street.

(fig. 70)

(fig. 71)

(figs. 70-75)
DOOR CAPITALS

The engaged columns that
support the entablature often
have Ionic capitals with
acanthus leaves, human heads
or swags:
(fig. 70) 79 O'Connell Street,
(fig. 71) 72 O'Connell Street,
(fig. 72) 4 The Crescent,
(fig. 73) 23 Barrington Street,
(fig. 74) 14 Barrington Street,
(fig. 75) 71 O'Connell Street.

(fig. 72)

(fig. 73)

(fig. 74)

(fig. 75)

(fig. 76)
BOOTSCRAPER
6 The Crescent

The terraces in the lower part of the town, from Rutland Street to mid-O'Connell Street and side streets, tend not to have basement areas and steps up to the ground floor. In some cases the basements have been filled in, but many still have basements, suggesting that the ground floors were designed as shops. There is a surviving sketch and several photographs of O'Connell Street tentatively dated to the late nineteenth century *(fig. 77)*. These show the shop formula to have been simple and fairly consistent. There was a narrow band at the top for the name, a tripartite division with vertically divided display windows between two doors. The window sections were divided by timber pilasters and given horizontal bands at the top, centre and base. Some windows had oval or arched divisions. Shopfronts, particularly vulnerable to fashion and decay, rarely survive, but there are a few, mainly on side streets. The pub on Augustinian Lane has an early nineteenth-century bow window, Tom Collins pub, Cecil Street, has its original tripartite divisioning, P. Deegan's, Denmark Street, its external shutters, and a shop on High Street had its fine wrought-iron window guard until very recently when the building was demolished.

(fig. 77)
GEORGE'S STREET
Photograph c.1870

This shows some of the shops erected in 1790s and 1800s in the lower part of George's Street (later O'Connell Street) between Thomas Street and Cecil Street.

Courtesy of Edward Chandler.

46 O'CONNELL STREET
c.1820

Detail of door. This building has an unusual early Gothic Revival shopfront with narrow vertical divisions to the window and fanlight and pointed arch details to the door.

3 LITTLE CATHERINE STREET
1827

A classically-inspired stucco composition.

3 LITTLE CATHERINE STREET

3 LITTLE CATHERINE STREET

(fig. 78)
1-6 PERY SQUARE
1836-39

View of Pery Square
Tontine by James Pain.

(fig. 79)
3 PERY SQUARE

Pery Square was designed by James Pain for the Pery Square Tontine Company (constituted to finance the building of the terrace) in 1834, and built between 1836 and 1839. It stands out because it was conceived as a stand-alone building, with a rusticated ashlar ground floor, a series of cast-iron first floor balconies, a heavy cornice and two advanced ends *(figs. 78-79)*. The entrances to houses 1 and 6 are at the sides and have porches, while the four remaining Greek Doric Revival entrances face the park.

The interiors of the new town terraces are more highly decorated than the exteriors. They reveal the high quality of the craftsmanship of Limerick joiners, plasterers and the makers of slate and marble fireplaces *(fig. 80)*. As with the exteriors there is consistency and responsiveness to status and hierarchy, but there is also inventiveness. In most houses the timber-panelled doors vary with position in the building: six panels for the first floor, five for the second and four for the third. There are usually pilaster-decorated arched openings between the hall and staircase and the front and back rooms on the ground and first floors. Most staircases have turned balusters on the main floors and plain balusters from the second to the top floor.

(fig. 80)
2 PERY SQUARE

The panels on the timber shutters often reflect the positions of the window mullions. Here elegance is achieved with no break in the shutter.

(fig. 82)
HARTSTONGE STREET
c.1830

Most houses display simple plaster cornicing, but some cornices are decorated with dentils, egg and dart and leaves, especially in the front hall *(fig. 81)*. There are many varieties of ceiling centrepiece usually displaying sprays of acanthus leaves, some dynamic and inventive *(figs. 82-83)*. There may also be radiating bands of wheat husks, garlands of flowers and scrolls, or vine leaves and grapes in an oval or circle. These designs can be found on hall, staircase, ground and first floor room ceilings and are particularly well preserved in the Chamber of Commerce building on O'Connell Street. Plain white or coloured marble fireplaces are normal in the larger houses on the first floor. Elsewhere slate fireplaces, larger and more elaborate on the lower floors, are usual. Halls were often floored in encaustic tiles *(fig. 84)*.

(fig. 81)
HARTSTONGE STREET
c.1830

Moulded plaster in relatively high relief.

(fig. 83)
2 PERY SQUARE
1836-39

Moulded plaster in
relatively high relief.

(fig. 84)
HARTSTONGE STREET

Encaustic tiles were often
used in halls.

**CHAMBER OF
COMMERCE**
96 O'Connell Street
c.1815-20

Ceiling plaster centrepieces
in low relief and of wide
radius.

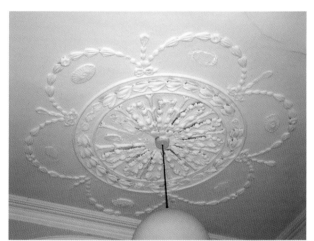

CHAMBER OF
COMMERCE
96 O'Connell Street

CHAMBER OF COMMERCE
96 O'Connell Street

This building has fine white
marble fireplaces in the two
first floor rooms. Both have
reeded colonettes supporting
mythological figures, and
carved centrepieces.

CHAMBER OF
COMMERCE
96 O'Connell Street

CHAMBER OF
COMMERCE
96 O'Connell Street

CHAMBER OF
COMMERCE
96 O'Connell Street

The round-headed landing
window is typical of
terraces in the new town.

CHAMBER OF COMMERCE
96 O'Connell Street

In most buildings the stair treads were carved in variations on a scroll. In the larger buildings, as here, more elaborate natural forms and swags may be seen.

CHAMBER OF COMMERCE
96 O'Connell Street

CHAMBER OF COMMERCE
96 O'Connell Street
c.1815-20

The Chamber of Commerce, instituted in 1815, moved to 96 O'Connell Street in 1829. The façade was stuccoed and French windows added c.1875.

(fig. 85)
SHANNON STREET
c.1790

This is the only surviving store in the river area. It has been sensitively restored and converted to apartments.

(fig. 86)
SHANNON STREET

(fig. 87)
53 THOMAS STREET
c.1870

A unique store built of
squared stone with ashlar
window surrounds, a
pediment, brick cornicing
and string courses.

The majority of the stone corn stores and mill buildings have gone, and with them the impression of Limerick as a working, industrial city, visible in old photographs. Most of the store and mill complexes that lined the river were pulled down in the 1960s *(figs. 85-86)*, but until recently there was a concentration of large (double-pitched roof) and smaller (single-pitched roof) stores in Robert Street and Denmark Street and in Old Windmill Road. Derelict corn stores surrounding a courtyard still stand at the top of Roches Street, and there is a fine block in Robert Street. Isolated stores can still be seen between the terraces *(fig. 87)*.

O'Connell Street. Showing Monument. Limerick.   M. 321.

(fig. 88)
THE CRESCENT
c.1823

The terraces were constructed by 1823. The statue to Daniel O'Connell by John Hogan, erected in 1857, further emphasises the neo-classical character of the double crescent.

Courtesy of the Irish Historical Picture Company.

(fig. 90)
FOUNTAIN
People's Park
1877

The two realised public spaces stand in the upper part of the new town. The Crescent is in fact a double crescent formed at the highest point of O'Connell Street *(fig. 88)*. Pery Square was envisaged on an 1827 map as an unclosed, Baroque square (New Square) on a continuation of Hartstonge Street. A monument was erected in 1831 *(fig. 89)* to Thomas Spring Rice, an MP for Limerick from 1820 to 1832, who represented the political interests of the merchants living and working in Newtown Pery. Shortly after the monument appeared the square was enclosed, and Pery Square was realised as a residential square on the London model. Only one side was completed. With the building of St Michael's Church near to the terrace and the enlarging of the square to become the People's Park in 1877 (with a cut stone entrance arch, bandstand and fountain *(fig. 90)*), Pery Square became synonymous with this quiet corner.

(fig. 89)
SPRING RICE MONUMENT
People's Park
1831

The statue was carved by Thomas Kirk. It stands at the top of a Doric column over 71 feet high (21.6m) designed by Henry Baker.

(fig. 91)
SARSFIELD BARRACKS
Lord Edward Street
1797-98

This image shows the parade ground. Rebuilt and altered after the fire in 1922, the barrack buildings retained the cut stone surrounds to the regularly placed round-headed doors. They also displayed projecting keystones and block-and-start, which was a feature typical of barracks and modest public buildings in late eighteenth-century Ireland.

Courtesy of Limerick City Museum.

(fig. 92)
SARSFIELD BARRACKS
Lord Edward Street

Detail of the stone wall plaque in the gatehouse.

Those who had escaped the restrictions of the Corporation oligarchy to build and work in Newtown Pery had formed themselves into an independent political group that lobbied parliament. They achieved a measure of separation from the Corporation with the Act of 1807 which provided for the formation of a body to levy a tax to administer St Michael's Parish. The resulting Commissioners of the Parish of St Michael provided lighting, cleaning, paving and a night-watch; they prevented encroachments on the street and supervised street repairs. They did not set down rules for urban design as the Wide Street Commissioners did in Dublin. In the absence of clauses specifying design or materials in the leases, it must be assumed that the consistency in the architecture of Newtown Pery resulted from the operation of a consensus.

The public buildings erected in the new town reflected the activities and preoccupations of the inhabitants: commerce, religion and leisure. They were modest buildings, whose positions were not part of the master plan, and which were not given particular prominence; in fact several of them were placed behind terraces, accessible by narrow lanes. The New Barracks (now Sarsfield Barracks) was built on a larger scale, but they were positioned on the southern edge of the new town and also had no civic presence. Built in 1797-8 by Graham Myers it was a typically austere collection of buildings built around a vast parade ground with a small pedimented gatehouse facing the Boherbuoy Road *(figs. 91-92)*.

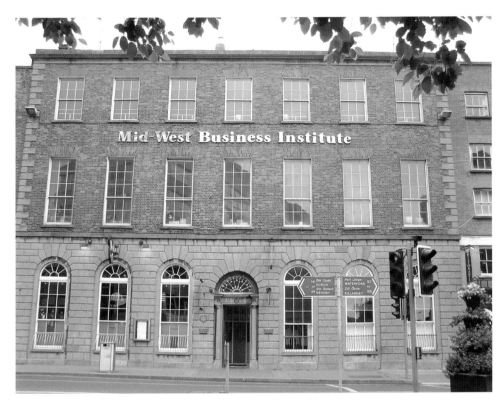

(fig. 93)
FORMER COMMERCIAL
BUILDINGS
Patrick Street
1805

This was the first head-
quarters of the Chamber of
Commerce and the place
where the Commissioners
of the Parish of St Michael
met. It fitted snugly into
the terrace, distinguished
by its rusticated stone
base, round-headed ground
floor windows, large scale,
heavy cornice, stone quoins
and unique door details.

The earliest public building to be inserted into the streets of the new town was the Commercial Buildings erected on Patrick Street in 1805 *(figs. 93-94)*. By 1840 there were a number of banks in the new town. The National Bank was a bow-ended building with a cut stone doorway on Sarsfield Street, and the Provincial Bank, designed by James Pain in 1839, has a cut stone façade and three pedimented windows. They are both terraced buildings, but the Savings Bank, designed by Thomas Deane in 1839, is a wonderful freestanding structure (though not given the axial position it deserves) and a full, if late, essay in Greek Revival design *(figs. 95-96)*.

(fig. 94)
FORMER COMMERCIAL
BUILDINGS
Patrick Street

Detail of carved lintel and
fanlight.

(fig. 95)
SAVINGS BANK
Glentworth Street
1839

Conceived as a temple with a Doric portico and beautiful blank side walls, it stands on a platform and delights with unexpected details such as the carved lions' heads and anthemions above the eaves.

(fig. 96)
SAVINGS BANK
Glentworth Street

Detail at the corner of the pediment, a lion's head and anthemion just visible at the top.

All the small Catholic chapels built before the Act of Catholic Emancipation in 1829 have been replaced by later nineteenth-century churches, with the exception of the Dominican Church on Baker Place, which was extended and remodelled both internally and externally in the mid-nineteenth century. There were at least seven non-conformist chapels, three of which still exist. The plainest of these, the Quaker Meeting House, accessed from Cecil Street, was built in 1806. It still has much of its original joinery, including a panelled balcony supported by cast-iron columns. Similar balconies and columns can be seen in the Presbyterian Meeting House on Glentworth Street, now a printing works and obscured by the later Pery Hotel *(fig. 97)*. Trinity Church, with its integral Ionic portico and pediment, was designed in conjunction with the Asylum for Blind Women on Catherine Street in 1834 *(fig. 98)*. The concentration of the Savings Bank, Presbyterian Chapel, Dominican Chapel and Trinity Church in the south-east corner of the new town (further public buildings and spaces would be added in the later nineteenth century) makes this an important area. The overhead wires, obtrusive signage and neglect to both buildings and public space, endemic in the entire new town area, is particularly deleterious here and prevents a full appreciation of its character.

(fig. 97)
McKERNS PRINTERS
(former Presbyterian Meeting House)
Glentworth Street
1846

Built in 1846 to replace an earlier building, it has a pedimented cut stone façade and doorway with inclined jambs that echo those of the Savings Bank opposite. The jambs are obscured by a later addition at ground floor level.

(fig. 98)
TRINITY CHURCH AND THE ASYLUM FOR BLIND FEMALES
(now the Health Service Executive Building)
Catherine Street
1834

The church was subsumed into the asylum building (to the left of the church) and the rectory (to the right) to produce a palace block.

Courtesy of the Knight of Glin.

Close by, in Pery Square, is St Michael's, the parish church, designed by James and George Pain in c.1836 to replace a chapel on O'Connell Street. Their elaborate Picturesque Gothick design was simplified in the execution, and when finished in 1844 looked more like a First Fruits church, though still heavily buttressed, pinnacled and crenellated *(figs. 99-100)*.

No early nineteenth-century buildings devoted to leisure remain, but there are two schools. The delightful, though not very accurate, brick Tudor Revival Leamy's Free School with crenellated central tower, octagonal chimneystacks and oriel windows, which opened in 1844, stands on Hartstonge Street *(fig. 101)*. In almost complete contrast Villiers Schools, of 1839, on Henry Street is an elegantly symmetrical classical block-with-wings composition in ashlar stone *(fig. 102)*.

(fig. 99)
ST MICHAEL'S CHURCH OF IRELAND CHURCH
Pery Square
c.1836

The tower was raised in 1877, giving the church a quiet authority and setting its stamp on Pery Square. The interior was remodelled in 1877 by William and Robert Fogarty when the chancel was added.

(fig. 100)
ST MICHAEL'S CHURCH OF IRELAND CHURCH
Pery Square

View of St Michael's in the context of Pery Square.

(fig. 101)
LEAMY HOUSE
(former Leamy's
Free School)
Hartstonge Street
1841-45

(fig. 102)
FORMER VILLIERS
SCHOOLS
Henry Street
1839

A beautifully detailed building, it has a bow-shaped portico supported by octagonal columns and recessed planes in the wings. The central block was originally an orphanage and school for Protestant girls, and the wings were day schools, one for boys and the other for girls.

LIMERICK PORT
Mid-twentieth century

This photograph, taken from the tower of St Mary's Cathedral at low tide, shows the migration of the port downstream. The remnants of the medieval port can be seen to the bottom right adjacent to the Potato Market. In the mid-eighteenth century trade centred around the Custom House to the middle left. Arthur's Quay and Honan's Quay in the centre of the photograph were built soon after. An act for a bridge and floating dock (at one time to be at Arthur's Quay) was passed in 1823. Wellesley Bridge (top right) and a small dock were opened in 1835. The port (far distance) was built further downstream in 1853.

Courtesy of Limerick City Museum.

SARSFIELD BRIDGE, LIMERICK.   R.810.

(fig. 103)
SARSFIELD BRIDGE
(former Wellesley
Bridge)
1824-35

Wellesley Bridge, named
after the viceroy, the
Marquis of Wellesley, was
partly financed through the
Commissioners of Public
Works and partly by the
rates and duties levied by
the Bridge Commissioners.

*Courtesy of Limerick City
Museum.*

From the early 1820s it was recognised that Limerick needed a floating dock and a new bridge that would enable the city to expand into County Clare where quarries, houses and quays were being established. Wellesley Bridge (now Sarsfield Bridge), a particularly graceful structure, as fine in its way as the Custom House, was designed by the engineer, Alexander Nimmo and completed in 1835 *(fig. 103)*. Several schemes for floating docks were proposed. The danger of flooding encouraged Limerick Bridge Commissioners (later Limerick Harbour Board) to acquire land further downstream at the edge of the new town. Construction work began in 1849 to provide employment during the Great Famine. The floating dock, constructed from vast blocks of local stone, was opened in 1853. A graving dock for repair work was completed in 1873.

THE QUAYS.LIMERICK. 5297.W.L.

STEAMBOAT QUAY

This photograph shows a passenger steamer leaving Limerick in about 1900 from Steamboat Quay. The docks were built just downstream from Steamboat Quay.

Courtesy of the National Library of Ireland.

Building outside Newtown Pery 1765-c.1840

ENGLISHTOWN

This late nineteenth-century view of Englishtown shows the late eighteenth- and nineteenth-century replacements and infill – breweries, mills, housing, Old County Goal and County Courthouse – which transformed the medieval town.

Courtesy of the National Library of Ireland.

ENGLISHTOWN

Nineteenth-century replacements of medieval structures in the north part of Englishtown include St Munchin's Church and Thomond Bridge. The riverside store opposite the castle inserted an element of Newtown Pery into this older corner of the city.

Courtesy of the National Library of Ireland.

Not all the building work in the ebullient era of the late eighteenth and early nineteenth century occurred in the new town. Where new building involved older institutions such as the Grand Jury and civil parishes, where building was initiated by government or where existing infrastructure was being upgraded, there was activity outside the grid, in the old towns and on green field sites. Many of these schemes were public buildings. During this period the general physical condition of the medieval city declined despite investment which integrated it into the new town.

When it was built in 1774 the House of Industry, a workhouse financed by the city and county Grand Juries, marked the beginning of public provision for the destitute *(fig. 104)*. An austere utilitarian structure with classical trimmings situated on the Clare side of the River Shannon, it set the general tone for later social institutions. It was replaced in 1841 (by which time it was chronically overcrowded) by the workhouse at Union Cross designed to standardised plans and specifications by George Wilkinson. One of 130 structures built in the wake of the Poor Law Act of 1838, it was an early example of a Victorian institution. It shared with the House of Industry a purposeful austerity and reliance on proportion and simplicity for aesthetic effect. Designed in a simplified domestic Tudor Revival style, it reflected the greater prevalence of revival styles of the mid- to late nineteenth century *(fig. 105)*.

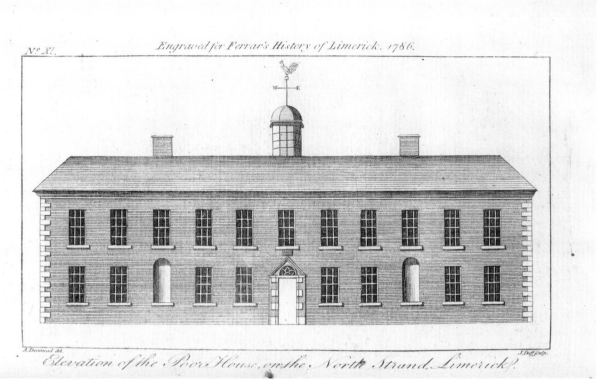

No. XI.　　　*Engraved for Ferrar's History of Limerick. 1786.*

A. Dunsead del.　　　*J. Duff sculp.*

Elevation of the Poor House, on the North Strand, Limerick.

(fig. 104)
HOUSE OF INDUSTRY
Clancy's Strand
1774

This view of the House of Industry is taken from the 1787 edition of John Ferrar's, *The History of Limerick*. By the early twentieth century the House of Industry was a barracks and had lost its pedimented door and cupola. Now it is converted into apartments.

Courtesy of the Leonard Collection, University of Limerick.

(fig. 105)
ST CAMILLUS'S
HOSPITAL
(former Limerick
Union Workhouse)
Shelbourne Road
1839-41

Built with split-faced stone walls contrasting with dressed stone details around the windows, door and at the gables, Limerick Workhouse relied on the masons' skill for aesthetic effect.

(fig. 106)
ST JOSEPH'S HOSPITAL
(former Limerick
District Asylum)
Mulgrave Street
1827

It was one of eight district asylums built in Ireland between 1823 and 1835 as a response to House of Commons Select Committee recommendations of 1817. The designs incorporated current reform principles often described as 'moral management'.

(fig. 107)
COUNTY GAOL
Mulgrave Street
1816-21

James Pain designed this gaol to replace the County Gaol on Merchant's Quay. This photograph shows the central administrative block above the entrance with two of the radiating cell blocks. The building has been subsequently modified.

Courtesy of the Tom Keogh Collection.

OLD COUNTY GAOL
Merchant's Quay
c.1789

Designed in c.1789 by William Blackburn, the entrance had more of a domestic than an institutional character, but it faced Merchant's Quay in a civic manner. Chronically overcrowded by 1814, it was demolished about twenty years ago.

Courtesy of Limerick City Museum.

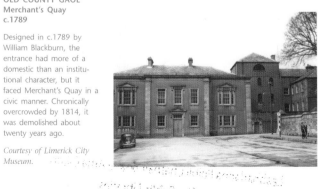

(fig. 108)
CITY HALL
(former City Gaol)
Crosbie Row
1813

The pedimented entrance with its recessed planes, the only part to survive, has a more institutional character than the old County Gaol.

By 1840 Mulgrave Street, a new road that ran south-east from Upper William Street in Newtown Pery, had become the location of a diverse collection of other early nineteenth-century institutions of mixed origins. There was the County Infirmary built in 1811 (now the Senior College), the Artillery Barracks of 1807 (of which only some fine pedimented cut stone façades remain), the County Gaol opened in 1821, and the Lunatic Asylum to which patients were first admitted in 1827. There was also a market complex opposite the barracks, now gone. The Gaol and the Asylum were both pioneering buildings, their designs owing much to rationally humane reforms proposed in Britain for the care and supervision of prisoners and lunatics. Both were purposefully geometric designs, employing a central administrative block influenced by Jeremy Bentham's Panopticon of 1791, which allowed a governor, unseen by the inmates, to have an uninterrupted view of the radiating arms which accommodated the inmates. The gaol, designed for the Grand Jury by James Pain, with its central decagonal tower and imposing stripped Doric entrance, is more forcefully an institution *(fig. 107)*. In the adjacent asylum the government-appointed architects, Francis Johnston and his nephew William Murray, could not conceal the scale of such a large institutional building in the adjacent asylum. But they could humanise the austerity through the use of domestic details in the gate lodges (now gone), by employing the country house formula for the two-storey central block, and by giving it a benign civic cupola *(fig. 106)*.

With the building of the new County Courthouse in 1809 on reclaimed land at the old port at right angles to the old County Gaol,

and the erection of a new City Gaol round the corner in 1813, the old centre of Limerick received a much-needed boost *(figs. 108-109)*. Both buildings were classical but more modest than many contemporary buildings of the same type, although the County Courthouse was aggrandised with a Tuscan portico in 1814. What was most remarkable was their prominent situation beside the Shannon. This was further enhanced after 1859 when the houses backing onto the cathedral graveyard were demolished, and a square, which extended to the Potato Market (built in 1844 over the medieval long dock), was opened up in front of them; it was spacious new town aesthetics inserted into the cramped quarters of the Englishtown.

(fig. 109)
COUNTY COURTHOUSE
Merchant's Quay
1809

The building is visible from both the River Shannon and the Abbey River. With its portico facing Merchant's Quay it reinforced the formality of the Old County Gaol. Still a courthouse, it has been recently refurbished, the interior modernised and controversial dormers inserted in the roof. This view shows the river front decorated on one side with limestone pilasters.

(fig. 110)
**ISLAND THEATRE
COMPANY
(former St Munchin's
Church of Ireland
Church)
Church Street
1827**

The church was
deconsecrated in 1968 and
restored as the headquar-
ters of the Island Theatre
Company. The original
Perpendicular window trac-
ery has gone, but the
ebonised gallery screen
and an internal door with
pointed arch decoration,
some later stained glass,
encaustic tiles and mural
monuments remain.

(fig. 111)
**ISLAND THEATRE
COMPANY
(former St Munchin's
Church of Ireland
Church)
Church Street**

Detail of the gallery screen.

In 1827 the north end of Englishtown was transformed by the replacing of the medieval St Munchin's Church with a modern structure, and the erection of almshouses and schools with money endowed by Hannah Villiers. Both were designed by James Pain and his brother, George, and built in squared rubble limestone. James Pain had been appointed architect to the Board of First Fruits for the ecclesiastical province of Cashel in 1822. Essentially a box and tower whose external decoration is confined to the hoodmouldings to the windows and the tower's prominent pinnacles, St Munchin's is a typical First Fruits church. Set in its ancient graveyard, it presides with grace over Englishtown *(figs. 110-111)*. With the almshouse and school complex the Pains employed the late medieval domestic (Tudor Gothic) style deemed appropriate for such buildings. The prominence of the many large diagonal stacks and dormers gives it a genuinely late medieval character, but the scale and symmetry of the whole and the way it faces a broad garden and the river, reflect early nineteenth-century tastes *(fig. 112)*.

(fig. 112)
VILLIERS ALMSHOUSES
Old Dominick Street
1827

Designed to accommodate Protestant widows in the central block, and with two schools in the wings, Villiers Almshouses is now used to house the elderly and has recently been restored. The quiet enclave retains its early nineteenth-century character.

James and George Pain were asked to design three bridges when trade revived in Limerick after the slump induced by the end of the Napoleonic Wars. By the mid-1820s the city, government and private interests wanted to improve the city's connection with its valuable agricultural hinterland. Athlunkard Bridge, completed in 1830 and connected to the new town by recently built roads, brought south and east Clare into the city's ambit. The narrow, dilapidated, building-encrusted fourteenth-century

Baal's Bridge was rebuilt in 1831 to connect Englishtown and Irishtown with a single efficient span *(fig. 113)*. Thomond Bridge, also declared to be beyond restoration, was rebuilt from 1836-1840 *(fig. 114)*. When, four years later, the Pains were asked to design a tollhouse for Thomond Bridge, they responded with the playful Picturesque style employing oversized battlemented parapets, bartizans and beautifully finished arrow-slits *(figs. 115-116)*.

(fig. 113)
BAAL'S BRIDGE
Mary Street/Broad
Street
1830-31

(fig. 114)
THOMOND BRIDGE
Castle Street/High Road
1840

Constructed with stone blocks having rough projecting faces, the bridge compliments the nearby thirteenth-century King John's Castle.

(fig. 115)
TOLLHOUSE
Verdant Place
1845

(fig. 116)
TOLLHOUSE
Verdant Place

Details of bartizan and arrow-slit.

Several hospitals were built in the old city during this period. Barrington's Hospital, started in 1829 by Matthew and Joseph Barrington and designed by the Dublin architect, Frederick Darley, has not only survived but, with its recent extension, has finally been completed *(fig. 117)*. In 1837 it was joined by a temple structure with a conspicuous dome. This was the Mont de Piété, a charitable pawn shop built to support the running costs of the hospital, which failed. The Mont de Piété was demolished in 1892.

The only building from this period to have survived in Irishtown is the Milk Market, which was a corn market in 1840. It is a unique open stone structure, recently restored, with a series of wide arched entrances (originally to an internal arcade) and a two-storey market house *(fig. 118)*. This was one of a number of market buildings and enclosures in the area just outside the medieval walls, including a two-storey Linen Hall. Only some patched perimeter walls now survive, in Ellen Street and Market Alley (now Little Ellen Street).

(fig. 118)
**MILK MARKET
Broad Street/Cornmarket
Street
c.1800**

The Broad Street and Cornmarket Street façades with the market house to the right.

(fig. 117)
**BARRINGTON'S
HOSPITAL
George's Quay
1829-30**

A classical building with an entrance loggia and undercroft and surviving nineteenth-century lamps. A partial attic, decorated with roundels, has been removed.

A glance at the 1840 Ordnance Survey map shows houses, each named, set in large gardens on the banks of the Shannon just beyond the city boundary. These are the villas built by successful businessmen in the early nineteenth century. Many of them still survive, as institutions or houses, in what are now more densely inhabited suburban areas. To the south-west are Laurel Hill (now a school), Ashbourne, and Summerville House (part of Mary Immaculate College). North of the river are houses on the North Circular Road, Shelbourne House (part of Ardscoil Rís), Tivoli (part of Villiers School) and Bellevue. These would later be joined by Sunville *(fig. 119)*, Kilmoyle *(fig. 120)*, Ardhu House (now an hotel) and Beechlawn. Within two arms of the river to the east are the villas of Mill Road. Most of these houses are elegant classical boxes with wide Italianate eaves and porticos. Some are a relaxed single-storey over basement, but others are of a more imposing two storeys, often with a central light well. There is usually a neat gate lodge and the gardens are surrounded by mature trees.

(fig. 120)
KILMOYLE
North Circular Road
c.1845

The Catholic Bishop's house until recently, Kilmoyle is built of sandstone with granite sills and portico.

(fig. 119)
SUNVILLE

This watercolour of Sunville by the artist John E. Bosanquet (fl.1854-61) shows Sunville without its later bay and with its rockery, croquet lawn and greenhouse.

Courtesy of Limerick City Museum.

Victorian Limerick

PATRICK STREET

This Lawrence photograph looks down Patrick Street towards Rutland Street. By the late nineteenth century many terraces in this area had become tenements.

Courtesy of the National Library of Ireland.

The population of the nineteenth-century city peaked at just over 66,500 before the Great Famine of 1845-9. After this disaster the population stood at 48,391 and numbers continued to fall slowly until the 1890s. During this time Limerick's industrial base decreased as factories and businesses declined or closed; the number of breweries, distilleries, corn mills, cotton and linen manufactories and tanneries had dropped even by the 1860s. Many people lived in great poverty, and during these years slum housing conditions spread from the old town to the lower end of Newtown Pery. When, in 1841, Limerick came within the operation of the Municipal Reform Act, which opened up the Corporation to new personnel, there was an opportunity for improvement. In 1853 the powers of the Commissioners of the Parish of St Michael were transferred to the Corporation, and the city was no longer divided. However, most subsequent developments, whether commercial, government sponsored or, very importantly for this period, ecclesiastical, still occurred in the new town or at its edges.

Alongside the general poverty in nineteenth-century Limerick there were success stories – John Norris Russell and Peter Tait are outstanding examples of businessmen who thrived during this period – and the middle class continued to grow. This did not result in a very big increase in the housing stock. Additions were confined to terraces and a few detached and semi-detached villas built on roads leading out of the city: O'Connell Avenue, South Circular Road, Ennis Road and Mulgrave Street *(fig. 121)*. Usually built of brick, sometimes with arched or bay windows, prone to brick detailing around doorcases, often with long front gardens, and nearly always with elaborate cast-iron railings, they displayed some of the new domestic fashions from England *(fig. 122)*. However, Georgian features and an un-Victorian restraint

(fig. 121)
ENNIS ROAD

Semi-detached houses and short terraces, each built in an individual style, and all with long front gardens, characterised this slowly growing suburb.

Courtesy of the National Library of Ireland.

(fig. 122)
MOYOLA TERRACE
Ennis Road
c.1880

The houses on this terrace have gabled bays and porches decorated with freestyle pediments, carved sandstone lintels and a mix of classical (dentils) and Gothic (finials) details.

(fig. 123)
BORU HOUSE
Mulgrave Street
1880

View of the front elevation
showing the polychromatic
brickwork and slates.

in the form of flat windows, fine joinery detailing and conservative plasterwork, remained longer in Ireland. One of the more exuberant houses, dated to 1880, is Boru House, the childhood home of the writer Kate O'Brien. It has polychromatic brick and slates, a bay window, decorative timber gates, unusual fretwork balusters to the staircase and the sculptured O'Brien emblem – a raised arm brandishing a sword – on the front gable *(figs. 123-124)*. Terraces of smaller workers' cottages were also built near the New Barracks and in the medieval suburb of Thomondgate (many survive), in the area east of the Englishtown walls (many recently demolished) and as replacements for dilapidated medieval houses in Irishtown (all demolished 20 years ago).

(fig. 124)
BORU HOUSE
Mulgrave Street

Detail of the highly
decorative timber gates.

Communications improved throughout Ireland in the mid-nineteenth century, especially with the building of the railways. By 1844 there was a regular train service between Limerick and Tipperary, which was extended to Waterford after 1854. Limerick Station, opened by 1858, possibly designed by Sancton Wood was, after great debate, situated on the eastern edge of Newtown Pery. It is a long, low, quietly civic building with three wide entrances that face Davis Street. This gives it a direct link with the new town, which is now diluted by a sea of cars in the forecourt *(fig. 125)*.

(fig. 125)
COLBERT STATION
Parnell Street
c.1858

Courtesy of the National Library of Ireland.

(figs. 126-127)
BORD GÁIS
Dock Road
c.1884

Details of the wall facing
the Dock Road.

(fig. 128)
BORD GÁIS
Dock Road

Detail of the arched opening in the interior wall.

(fig. 129)
LANSDOWNE FLAX MILL
North Circular Road

(fig. 131)
LANSDOWNE FLAX MILL
North Circular Road

(fig. 130)
LANSDOWNE FLAX MILL
North Circular Road
1853

Lansdowne flax mill later
became a condensed milk
factory run by Cleeves and
is still used to process liq-
uid milk. It is constructed
of squared limestone blocks
with beautifully detailed
ashlar surrounds to the
windows. However, it is
most remarkable for its
semi-circular end with its
curved cornice.

Several industrial structures of the mid-Victorian period survive. Gas was introduced to light the streets of the new town in 1824 and the United General Gas Company moved to the newly built Dock Road in 1884. Two interesting walls from the main building remain: one on the interior of the site has three highly placed semi-circular openings with vermiculated voussoirs *(fig. 128)*; the other, which faces the road, has six round-headed arches at one end and a dramatic segmental arch at the other end, all blocked *(figs. 126-127)*. Nearby stands the remains of a power station with split-face stone gables and a cast-iron roof that was clad in glass until recently. On the other side of the river John Norris Russell built Lansdowne flax spinning and weaving mill, a large four-storey factory with a vast perimeter wall and outbuildings, which was in operation by 1853 *(figs. 129-131)*. Tait's Army Clothing Factory, situated near the New Barracks, was a significant employer in mid-nineteenth-century Limerick, but only the entrance gate and some burnt-out shells survive of the 1850s complex on Edward Street.

(fig. 132)
BANNATYNE MILLS
Dock Road
1874

View of Bannatyne Mills from the dock. With its machicolated tower and batter, it had a castellated theme. Inside it was the most advanced corn mill in Ireland in 1874. It was designed by William Cox.

(fig. 133)
BANNATYNE MILLS
Dock Road

(fig. 134)
BANNATYNE MILLS
Dock Road

All of these buildings rely on the great versatility and craftsmanship of the local stone masons who, by the mid-nineteenth century, were adept at making rock-face and split-face blocks, tooled, punched and hammer-dressed ashlar. They were accomplished in laying rubble in various styles: squared and coursed, random rubble coursed and uncoursed, with skew vertical joints, or with snecks. Bannatyne Mills, a state-of-the-art corn mill with a cast-iron frame, designed by the architect and engineer William Cox and opened at the new docks in 1874, differed from other mill buildings in its use of cast-iron internal columns and stone cladding that was more self-consciously architectural *(figs. 132-134)*.

(fig. 135)
MODEL SCHOOL
O'Connell Avenue
1855

The Model School, although opened in 1855, was the result of earlier nineteenth-century reform initiatives. The Tudor/Jacobean style with details such as the four-centred arch, finials and label mouldings to some openings, was a vernacular style when applied in southern England but stood out as a new revived style in Ireland.

(fig. 136)
MODEL SCHOOL
O'Connell Avenue

As the nineteenth century progressed a greater variety of historic architectural styles were revived and applied for symbolic purposes. The Model Schools on O'Connell Avenue, opened in 1855, one of over 16 built by the Board of National Education, was designed by Frederick Darley in an understated Tudor/ Jacobean style. This had become established in Britain as appropriate for schools, largely because it allied nineteenth-century reforms with the expansion in education in the sixteenth and seventeenth centuries *(figs. 135-136)*.

The symbolic value of architectural style was particularly appreciated by the churches, both Catholic and Protestant, and their architects. The Board of First Fruits had favoured a pared down Gothic for Church of Ireland churches, but when John Welland became architect to the Board's successor, the Ecclesiastical Commissioners, he pioneered a simple Hiberno-Romanesque style as a replacement for medieval St John's in Irishtown in 1843. He also indicated a debt to A.W.N. Pugin by roofing nave, apse, and aisles separately and revealing the roof structure *(fig. 137)*.

The Catholic Church began a revolutionary building programme in the mid-century which had a momentum that would carry it well into the twentieth century. The friary chapels and parish church within Newtown Pery, all of which still stand, were gradually rebuilt and furnished as money, much of it from parish collections, became available. Meanwhile, orders of nuns, the Christian Brothers and the missionary Redemptorists became established on the outskirts of the city. Gothic continued to be the favoured style in the 1850s, but in the 1860s and 70s it was largely superseded by classical styles which underlined the church's connections with Rome. Later, under the influence of the late nineteenth-century Celtic Revival, and as a sign of the antiquity of the Catholic Church in Ireland, the Church would adopt the Hiberno-Romanesque style.

One of the first eighteenth-century chapels to be rebuilt was St John's. The new church was designed by Philip Charles Hardwick and opened in 1861, not as a church, but as a cathedral. Even more than Welland's nearby church it owed much to Pugin, being Early English Gothic and inspired by Killarney Cathedral.

Inside, the high rood screen with its images of Christ crucified, the Virgin and St John, gives the church a medieval tone to which the Church of Ireland revivalists never quite aspired. The spire, satisfyingly elaborate, which soars over the city, was built later by M.A. Hennessy *(fig. 138)*. Contemporary with St John's was the church and monastery of the Redemptorists on South Circular Road dedicated to St Alphonsus Liguori *(figs. 139-140)*. The interior, like many Catholic interiors, has no east window and an organ obstructs the west window. Richly decorated tabernacles and altars, chancel and chapel furnishing were completed piecemeal, as elsewhere, over the succeeding decades. The chief charm of St Alphonsus lies in the beautifully lit side chapels with their stained glass roofs and flower mosaics, in George Goldie's reredos of 1865 and the golden Oppenheimer apse mosaics of 1927 *(fig. 141)*.

(fig. 137)
ST JOHN'S CHURCH OF IRELAND CHURCH
Church Street
1843

Built in a simple Hiberno-Romanesque revival style, the church has a round-arched door, not unlike the early medieval church at Kilrush, County Limerick, billet moulding to define wall panels, and cushion capitals to the columns. The careful use of stone texture and shade adds depth to the design.

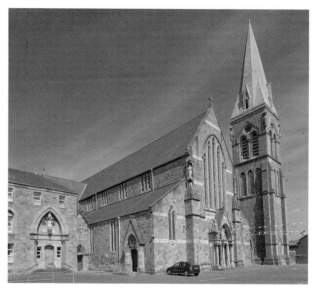

(fig. 139)
ST ALPHONSUS LIGUORI REDEMPTORIST CHURCH
South Circular Road
1858

Designed by Philip Charles Hardwick it is Early English Gothic in style with a touch of Ruskinian colour with the bands of pink granite in the limestone. The tower and spire, designed by George Goldie and less ambitious than the one designed by Hardwick, was completed in 1875.

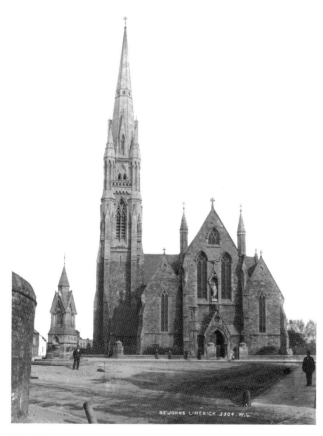

(fig. 138)
ST JOHN'S ROMAN CATHOLIC CATHEDRAL
Cathedral Place
1855-61

Courtesy of the National Library of Ireland.

(fig. 140)
ST ALPHONSUS LIGUORI REDEMPTORIST CHURCH
South Circular Road

(fig. 141)
ST ALPHONSUS LIGUORI
REDEMPTORIST CHURCH
South Circular Road

St Gerard's Chapel,
decorated with stained
glass and wall mosaics.

(fig. 142)
FRANCISCAN CHURCH
Henry Street
1876-86

The Franciscan Church, which has the largest portico in Limerick, dominates the foot of Henry Street.

The executant architect for the church of St Alphonsus was William Edward Corbett (it was designed by P.C. Hardwick), architect and borough surveyor for Limerick City from 1854-c.1899. Much of his work was in altering and adding, though he designed a few country Gothic churches. His big chance came with the city's Franciscan Friary, whose foundation stone was laid in 1876. He designed a rectangular basilica with Corinthian capitals loosely based on Santa Maggiore in Rome *(fig. 142)*. The later apse (to his design) is decorated with marbles of a warm burnt sienna, which complement the Roman character of the nave. The Jesuits also designed a classical church. Although uncomfortably inserted into the Crescent it has a light interior enhanced by a

(fig. 143)
**CHURCH OF THE
SACRED HEART**
The Crescent
1864-67

Surprisingly light and
sumptuously decorated, the
church was recently sold
and the contents auc-
tioned.

*Courtesy of the Copper Reed
Studio, Limerick.*

(fig. 144)
**CHURCH OF THE
SACRED HEART**
The Crescent

Detail of tabernacle.

*Courtesy of the Copper Reed
Studio, Limerick.*

CHURCH OF THE
SACRED HEART
The Crescent

The lower wall of the apse
was walled in Italian marble while the upper was
decorated with mosaics
depicting Jesuit saints.

(fig. 145)
**CHURCH OF THE
SACRED HEART
The Crescent**

Detail of altar.

*Courtesy of the Copper Reed
Studio, Limerick.*

fine neo-classical altar, beautifully coloured marbles, interesting mosaics and the remains of its pre-Vatican II marble altar rail *(figs. 143-145)*. Some of these beautifully crafted features have been removed since its sale. The parish church of St Michael, located at the lower end of the new town at the foot of Chapel Lane, is memorable for its gentle tower topped with a golden statue of St Michael. Built to replace an earlier chapel in 1881, it was an early Catholic Hiberno-Romanesque church, though designed with far less feeling for the style than Welland's St John's Church.

Unfortunately the Sisters of Mercy Convent of 1852 on King's Island has recently been demolished. Its plastered classical façade and gateway were well sited at the bottom of the wide road opposite the castle, and its simple stone tower was visible from the canal. At Mount St Vincent on O'Connell Avenue the Sisters of Mercy chose Gothic for their convent, orphanage and chapel whose spire is prominent in the area *(fig. 146)*. The Good Shepherd Convent on the Dublin Road has been acquired by the Limerick School of Art and Design, and its distinctively domed church, lined with gold and pale coloured mosaic and decorated plaster, has been converted into an art gallery.

During the nineteenth century the commercial streets of Newtown Pery gradually changed as shops upgraded their premises by replacing their narrow windows with plate glass, adding stucco to their façades and redesigning their shopfronts. Number 112 O'Connell Street still has stuccoed pilasters with Corinthian capitals and vermiculated quoins. Number 16 William Street, an office, has a decorative scheme in which stucco and cast-iron nicely complement each other. James Gleeson, a pub on O'Connell Street, has a late nineteenth-century shopfront and cast-iron lamps. Cast-iron cresting can be seen above W.J. South's on Newenham Street.

Several department stores were built on O'Connell Street, Cannock's and Todd's being the most celebrated. These have long gone, but a surviving building on the corner of Ellen Street and Patrick Street indicates how magnificent these buildings could be *(fig. 147)*. Terracotta was not common in Limerick, but there are two buildings with terracotta details in William Street; numbers 11-12 is a particularly handsome building with fine terracotta detail designed in c.1865 by William Fogarty. There were several new bank buildings in Victorian Limerick: what is now the Ulster Bank on one corner of Glentworth Street and O'Connell Street is a stuccoed terrace building (with a later Edwardian classical entrance), while the Bank of Ireland on the opposite corner is a purpose-built structure, curved at the corner, and faced in stone.

(fig. 146)
MOUNT ST VINCENT CONVENT
O'Connell Avenue
1851

(fig. 147)
9-11 PATRICK STREET/ ELLEN STREET
1872

Inspired by Venetian palazzi, the shop has carved stone pilasters to the three floors and red granite columns to the arched openings on the first floor.

GEORGE'S STREET

View down George's Street towards the clock tower of Cannocks. Victorian lamp stands, carved stone (including small figures on a music shop) and stucco, and decorated cast-iron balconies give the street a prosperous character.

Courtesy of the National Library of Ireland.

(fig. 148)
ATHENAEUM
Cecil Street
1856

Like the Commercial
Building of 1805, the
Athenaeum is a distinctive
public building that fits into
the pattern of terraces: in
this case it is the pediment
and ground floor pilasters
which distinguish it.

(fig. 149)
BAKER PLACE

The Protestant Orphan
Society Hall to the left of
the Tait Clock is Gothic in
spirit as well as detail. It is
asymmetrical, has a steeply
pitched roof and is based
on the medieval hall. The
clock is a Victorian Gothic
confection. The ungainly
Havergal Hall, built in 1840
for the Limerick
Philosophical and Literary
Society, has now gone.

*Courtesy of the National
Library of Ireland.*

The several lecture theatres and club houses set up in Newtown Pery in the early nineteenth century have gone, but the Athenaeum Building, designed with a lecture theatre and opened on Cecil Street in 1856, still stands *(fig. 148)*. The Protestant Orphan Society Hall, designed by William Fogarty in 1865, is an example of secular Gothic Revival applied to a charity building *(fig. 149)*. It faces Baker Place, which received a focus two years later when the Gothic Revival clock tower in memory of Peter Tait was built. Other expressions of Victorian civic pride were added throughout the period: a statue of Viscount FitzGibbon on Sarsfield Bridge (1855), the O'Connell monument in the Crescent (1857), a fountain at the entrance to St John's Square (1865), a cut stone pedestal (1865) for the stone on which the Treaty of Limerick is said to have been signed, an Italianate clock (1880) for the docks *(figs. 150-151)* and a romantic statue (1881) of Patrick Sarsfield outside St John's Cathedral.

(fig. 150)
LIMERICK DOCKS
1880

Italianate elegance set with Victorian optimism in the docks.

(fig. 151)
LIMERICK DOCKS

Edwardian Limerick

VERONA VILLAS
O'Connell Avenue
c.1910

The careful use of contrasting materials – limestone,
pebbledash and brick –
probably owes something
to Clifford Smith. This terrace still has its Art
Nouveau inspired railings.

ARDCAOIN
O'Connell Avenue
c.1905

Ardcaoin is a fine, isolated
example of Edwardian neo-
Georgian domestic design
with the oversized details
that the Edwardians knew
how to handle.

In terms of style the Edwardian period (1890-1914) is a distinctive, ebullient episode that is moderately well represented in Limerick. Applied to speculative housing, one-off suburban houses and urban churches, the Edwardian style gave a new flavour to Victorian building types. The late nineteenth century had seen government-led initiatives in higher education, library provision and the postal service, and the resulting buildings can be defined as Edwardian in scope as well as style. Developments in leisure and commerce at this period also required some new types of building that can still be found in Limerick.

Edwardian suburban houses on O'Connell Avenue, Ennis Road and Shelbourne Road are of broadly two types. There are those which, at three storeys and sporting an assortment of balconies, oculi, porches and timbered gables, are brashly confident and stylistically eclectic *(figs. 152-154)*. Others, with horizontal mullioned windows, steeper and sometimes multiple roofs and prominent chimneys, owe much to the Arts and Crafts style with its domestic medieval roots. These appear more subtly confident. Most were large houses designed for the middle class, but there are enclaves of smaller houses such as the simple, symmetrically conceived Verona Esplanade off O'Connell Avenue.

ARDCAOIN
O'Connell Avenue

(fig. 153)
**NAOMH IOSAF, MAYFAIR
AND GLENADE**
O'Connell Avenue
c.1900

Bright with the Edwardian
combination of orange
brick and light stone
details, these houses also
display their original fenestration with its play on the
square and arch.

(fig. 152)
**MORAVAN AND
ROSSARD**
Ennis Road
c.1910

White painted timber and
balconies give these houses
a more open and pleasant
aspect than their Victorian
predecessors.

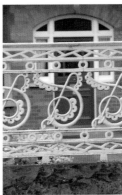

(fig. 154)
**NAOMH IOSAF, MAYFAIR
AND GLENADE**
O'Connell Avenue

(fig. 155)
SHANNON
ROWING CLUB
Sarsfield Bridge
1902

It is a measure of the success of the design that such a prominent domestic building sits at ease in its wide river and urban setting.

(fig. 156)
BELLTABLE ARTS
CENTRE
O'Connell Street
1919

Designed by Clifford Smith, it was originally the Gaiety Cinema, converted from a Georgian terrace building.

This Edwardian freestyle had been given impetus in Limerick in 1902 when the inventive young English architect Clifford Smith won an international competition to design the Shannon Rowing Club on a man-made island connected to Sarsfield Bridge *(fig. 155)*. His mark is evident in both the large-scale massing of the building with its gables, bays and balconies, and in the small details such as the Art Nouveau repoussée metal finger plates on the interior doors. Asymmetry and the enlargement of features such as corbels, brackets, arches and columns are particularly attractive features of Edwardian design. Clifford Smith executed both with panache in the design for the façade of the Gaiety Cinema (now the Belltable Arts Centre) on O'Connell Street with its bold elliptical arch and mannered columns *(figs. 156-157)*.

(fig. 157)
BELLTABLE ARTS
CENTRE
O'Connell Street

Edwardian freestyle of a more domestic character was applied to two small commercial buildings in the vicinity of the docks. The Guinness office on O'Curry Street has a bay windowed façade enlivened with a classical theme, while the single-storey National Rusks building on the Dock Road, originally commissioned by a Scottish company, has references to Scottish vernacular building with its projecting stepped chimneystack *(fig. 158)*.

(fig. 158)
DOCK ROAD
c.1910

(fig. 159)
GENERAL POST OFFICE
Henry Street
1903

This symmetrical extension to the post office, designed by T.J. Mellon, has diocletian windows and a Baroque Revival doorcase with the royal insignia of Edward VII carved in the pediment.

(fig. 160)
GENERAL POST OFFICE
Henry Street

(fig. 161)
GENERAL POST OFFICE
Henry Street

For the institutional buildings of the period designers often made more consistent references to historical styles. The Office of Public Works instituted a post office building programme in about 1891. The former temperance hall on the corner of Henry Street and Cecil Street, with its terracotta and its awkward combination of oriel window and semi-circular opening, may date to this period. Next to it is a more assured building with Baroque Revival details dated to 1903 *(figs. 159-161)*. The Carnegie Library, designed by George P. Sheridan, was built next to the People's Park in 1906. Sheridan used a Celtic Revival influenced Hiberno-Romanesque for the doorway and continued the theme with round-headed windows *(fig. 162)*. The period saw the building of a number of technical institutes. Limerick's, designed in 1909 by the London architect W.P. Ryan, is like many, Queen Anne Revival in style. It has vertically treated façades, arched windows, a flamboyant doorway and a broken roofline pediment *(figs. 163-164)*.

(fig. 162)
**LIMERICK CITY ART GALLERY
(former Carnegie Library)
Pery Square
1906**

A rare instance of ecclesiastical Hiberno-Romanesque applied to a civic building with a cupola and the Edwardian feeling for asymmetry. The stained glass above the door was made in the An Túr Gloine studios.

(fig. 163)
**MUNICIPAL TECHNICAL
INSTITUTE**
O'Connell Avenue
1909

This building is in the
Queen Anne Revival style,
with an exuberant
Baroque pedimented win-
dow which breaks the
roofline.

(fig. 164)
**MUNICIPAL TECHNICAL
INSTITUTE**
O'Connell Avenue

Two asymmetrical Gothic Revival non-conformist churches, each with a strong street presence, have a definite Edwardian character in which their asymmetry owes more to the desire to create an interesting public façade than to Puginian dictates. The Baptist Church, built in 1894 on Quinlan Street, is more functionally explicit. The Presbyterian Church, built five years later on Henry Street, displays the Edwardian combination of brick and stone and has Arts and Crafts influenced iron railings *(fig. 165)*. The Catholic Church, meanwhile, continued to commission revival buildings in the Victorian idiom: St Joseph's, designed by W.E. Corbett, and opened next to the Baptist Church in 1904, is a classical design, while St Mary's, Athlunkard Street by Ashlin and Coleman, opened in 1932, and the Augustinian Church on O'Connell Street, of 1942, were designed in what had become the popular Hiberno-Romanesque style.

(fig. 165)
HOWARTH, BASTOW
AND CHARLESTON
(former Presbyterian
Church)
Lower Mallow Street/
Henry Street
1899-1901

Designed by George
Ashlin, the church is
constructed in Ruabon
red brick and Portland
stone.

After Independence

(fig. 166)
ISLAND FIELD
King's Island
1934

The Island Field Housing scheme, built in 1934 on what had become known as King's Island, was one of the first public housing schemes to be built in Limerick after the Housing Acts of 1931-2.

One of the main priorities of the new state was the eradication of slums and the provision of social housing. This was inaugurated with the Housing Acts of 1931-2, and for the next fifty years large areas of Limerick beyond the modest suburban development of the nineteenth and early twentieth centuries were covered with estates of simple, box-like houses. Their construction, in mass concrete or concrete block and cavity walls, and cement roof slates, owed much to the revolution in the building industry. Aesthetically they are severely reduced, economic versions of the Edwardian domestic style *(fig. 166)*.

It was during the thirties that the great move away from revivalism pioneered in Europe before the First World War and known, after 1932, as the International Style began to appear in Ireland. There are few examples of well-conceived International Style or modern movement buildings in Limerick. However, because of the new technology on which the aesthetic rested, and the adoption of some of its stylistic quirks and details, it is apparent in most publicly funded and commercial projects executed during the mid-twentieth century. The lack of quality is something that occurred throughout Ireland at this time and was largely due to relative poverty; new buildings had to be built as economically as possible.

International Style houses with flat roofs, white rendered walls and horizontal fenestration were built in Corbally and the South Circular Road. Longville with its corner windows and cubic form is a particularly interesting example *(figs. 167-168)*. St Anne's Vocational School, built in 1939, on George's Quay has an undistinguished diluted modernist

(fig. 167)
LONGVILLE
South Circular Road
c.1940

An International Style
house in a middle class
suburb.

(fig. 168)
LONGVILLE
South Circular Road

(fig. 169)
LIMERICK SCHOOL OF
ART AND DESIGN
(former St Anne's
Vocational School)
George's Quay
1939

A structure made
interesting by period details
such as stepped stone
roundel detailing on the
brick piers of the external
railings, octagonal newel
with integral lamp and the
use of terrazzo inside.

(fig. 170)
LIMERICK SCHOOL OF
ART AND DESIGN
(former St Anne's
Vocational School)
George's Quay

Detail of newel, lamp and
terazzo.

exterior with brick detailed horizontal windows in a rendered façade. However, in the entrance hall the two-storey rear bow, the use of terrazzo for walls and floor, and the horizontal metal rails of the staircase, with its octagonal metal lamp, are all period details of quality *(figs. 169-170)*. The maternity hospital on the Ennis Road, built in 1960, has a similar brick and rendered façade. Its horizontal character however, is derived from the use of balconies, well established by then as desirable for hospitals, and also by the bars on its vertical windows *(fig. 171)*. St Munchin's Girls' primary school, designed by Andrew Devane and built in 1955 on the new estate of Moylish, is a more thorough-going and inventive essay in modernism, and was influenced by Frank Lloyd Wright *(fig. 172)*. This is evident in the flowing interior spaces, the massing of flat and curved roof elements, the separation of planes and the

(fig. 171)
LIMERICK REGIONAL
MATERNITY HOSPITAL
Ennis Road
1960

Balconies were well
established for health
buildings by the mid-twentieth century.

(fig. 172)
ST MUNCHIN'S GIRLS'
NATIONAL SCHOOL
Moylish Road
1955

A strikingly dynamic and
innovative building in its
external form, interior
space and use of materials.

(fig. 173)
**ST MUNCHIN'S GIRLS'
NATIONAL SCHOOL**
Moylish Road

View of the main hall.
Dynamic modernism is
seen in the angled walls
and the clear visual separation between the walls
and ceiling.

(fig. 174)
**ST MUNCHIN'S GIRLS'
NATIONAL SCHOOL**
Moylish Road

Detail of cast-profiled
concrete blocks.

(fig. 175)
SARSFIELD HOUSE
Francis Street
1970

Sarsfield House, the most prominent of the 1970s office blocks, is a formidable eighteen-bay seven-storey block adjacent to the Hunt Museum. It is clad in concrete panels and its concrete frame is exposed at the base in Corbusian style. It replaced warehouses which had a similar presence on the river.

experimental use of cast-profiled concrete blocks *(figs. 173-174)*. A few years earlier Devane had designed the dormitory wing to Mary Immaculate College (first built in 1899) where he pioneered the use of stair towers in Limerick and employed coloured glass. The designer of the c.1950 extension to the post office on Lower Cecil Street opted for a vertical emphasis for this city centre site with curtain wall glazing and integral panelling for the large central hall. Relative prosperity in the 1960s and 70s resulted in a number of bland office blocks using steel or concrete frames and repeated window modules in a horizontal pattern *(fig. 175)*.

The celebration of function was one of the tenets of modernism. It is most readily applied to industrial buildings, and can be seen in Limerick in the Bannatyne (later Ranks) silo built at the docks in 1935 *(fig. 176)*. A multi-storey building (originally one of two) with windows for the ground-floor offices and ventilation oculi at parapet level, the vast walls in between have no openings, but are articulated by the vertical concrete piers of the structure *(fig. 177)*. The Church of Our Lady of the Rosary, designed by Frank Corr and Liam McCormick and built in 1951, expresses the functions of the pre-Vatican II liturgy in the traditional way. However, constructed from a light steel frame and clad in timber weather-boarding with clerestory windows running the entire length of the building, it seems the epitome of modern functionalism *(figs. 178-180)*.

(fig. 176)
BANNATYNE (LATER RANKS) SILO
Dock Road
1935

The remaining Ranks silo seen next to Bannatyne's Mill from across the floating dock.

(fig. 177)
BANNATYNE (LATER RANKS) SILO
Dock Road

Although an unadorned structure with the functions of the interior spaces expressed on the exterior, the vertical division into base, centre and top reflects the divisions of classical architecture.

(fig. 178)
OUR LADY OF THE ROSARY ROMAN CATHOLIC CHURCH
Ennis Road
1951

One of the first modernist ecclesiastical structures to be constructed in the state, this church was intended to be a temporary building. Now the fine timber campanile, settled among mature trees, is a familiar and well-loved landmark on the Ennis Road.

(fig. 179)
OUR LADY OF THE ROSARY ROMAN CATHOLIC CHURCH
Ennis Road

(fig. 180)
OUR LADY OF THE ROSARY ROMAN CATHOLIC CHURCH
Ennis Road

Urban commercial buildings were often designed in a stripped classical style, or with reference to the decorative Art Deco style, which became popular in the 1930s. Limerick's examples are modest. Roches Stores (now Debenhams), which opened at the junction of O'Connell Street and Sarsfield Street after 1937, displays a stripped classicism inflected with Art Deco on the fluted piers that rise from the first to third storey. The first floor and pedimented parapet of the nearby ACC Bank building is a good example of a more exuberant Art Deco with a Greek theme *(figs. 181-182)*.

(fig. 181)
ACC BANK
131 O'Connell Street
1941

Classicism given an Art Deco twist: the shape of the pediment and the style of the lettering gives the context in which the large anthemion and Greek key frieze seem almost jazzy.

(fig. 182)
ACC BANK
131 O'Connell Street

Conclusion

HENRY STREET

View up Henry Street with the converted corn store set in the context of office, commercial and residential blocks designed by Carr Associates and Carr Cotter Naessens.

HENRY STREET

View down Henry Street towards the Franciscan Church, with a converted corn store to the right. The monumental modernism of Dunnes Stores was designed by Newenham Mulligan, the practice originally set up by Clifford Smith in the early twentieth century.

Limerick is still defined by the Shannon, running majestically through what is an expanding city. Visually the river is the core of the city, and it is from the river that the natural setting of Limerick and its historical development can most easily be appreciated.

Nothing of the congestion and inward-looking character of the medieval walled city remains. Instead, it is the monumental castle and cathedral, both radically altered since their foundation, which remind us of medieval Limerick. One characteristic medieval form, the uncoursed rubble limestone wall, using local

RIVERPOINT

View up the River Shannon from the docks towards King's Island. Contemporary development is proceeding at an ever increasing scale with Riverpoint the most recent building, being built at sixteen storeys. In places this threatens older small-scale buildings unless their context is protected. This is the case with the County Courthouse, which stands out on its spur of reclaimed land on King's Island above Sarsfield Bridge.

RIVERPOINT

View from the old dock at Sarsfield Bridge down river. The quays have been transformed and they are now a contemporary window to the river. There are plans to develop this area as a place to walk and enjoy the physical beauty of Ireland's greatest river.

quarried stone, survives patchily. But, as a staple for boundary walls and the external walls of many structures until the early twentieth century, it has given the city much of its character and its beguiling sense of place.

The character and the influence of the Georgian new town is still of central importance to Limerick. Newtown Pery soon became the commercial and cultural centre of Limerick, as it still is today, and its spacious, red brick terrace-lined grid is the essence of the city. The effect of this early nineteenth-century urbanism is best seen from O'Connell Street, although its splendour is severely compromised by prevalent decay, intrusive signage, overhead wires and parked cars. The early nineteenth-century city is still evident beyond the grid where many of the new institutional buildings were erected. The medieval towns were also transformed in the nineteenth century, in many cases by structures designed by James and George Pain, who have arguably made the greatest contribution to the city's architecture. The later nineteenth and early twentieth century was a period of consolidation and cautious expansion. Much of the extensive ecclesiastical and commercial building of this period remains, but its industrial character has largely been eradicated.

It would take an aerial view to give a full impression of contemporary Limerick. Steady early twentieth-century growth has recently become a rapid expansion up to and beyond county boundaries, leading to debate about the need for boundary extension. In the centre there has been huge commercial growth driven by government-led urban renewal schemes involving both new build, the upgrading of existing structures (such as the County Courthouse), the reuse of old buildings (most successfully the Hunt Museum) but also, unfortunately, much demolition. A start has been made to re-orientate the city towards the river, most dramatically with two high-rise blocks. Some of the recent office development on Henry Street displays an exemplary urbanism, contemporary in character but sensitive to existing buildings. Meanwhile the historic core faces a number of threats. Peripheral commercial development challenges the viability of the centre, while the compensating drive for city centre development tends to favour new build over the reuse of old. The contemporary challenge for Limerick, as elsewhere, is to attract development and encourage innovation while also implementing a programme of conservation to maintain a vital link with the past.

Further Reading

Aalen, F.H.A., Kevin Whelan and Matthew Stout, eds, *Atlas of the Irish Rural Landscape* (Cork, 1997).

Becker, Annette, John Olley and Wilfried Wang, eds, *20th-Century Architecture Ireland* (Munich, 1997).

Bence-Jones, Mark, *Burkes's Guide to Country Houses*, vol. 1, Ireland (New York, 1978).

Clarke, Howard B., ed., *Irish Cities* (Cork and Dublin, 1995).

Craig, Maurice, *Classic Irish Houses of the Middle Size* (London, 1976).

Craig, Maurice, *The Architecture of Ireland from earliest times to 1880* (London, 1989).

FitzGerald, Desmond, Knight of Glin, 'A Baroque Palladian in Ireland, the architecture of Davis Duckart, I', *Country Life*, vol. 142, no. 3682, 28th Sept. 1967, pp.735-739.

FitzGerald, Desmond, Knight of Glin, 'The last Palladian in Ireland, the architecture of Davis Duckart, II', *Country Life*, vol. 142, no. 3683, 5th Oct. 1967, pp.798-801.

FitzGerald, Desmond, Knight of Glin, 'Georgian Limerick', *Bulletin of the Irish Georgian Society*, III, no. 4, Oct.-Dec. 1960, pp.33-46.

Foster, Roy, ed., *The Oxford Illustrated History of Ireland* (London, 1991).

Franklin, Margaret, *A bibliography of Limerick city and county* (Doon, 2005).

Grimes, Brendan, *Irish Carnegie Libraries* (Dublin, 1998).

Hill, Judith, *The Building of Limerick* (Cork and Dublin, 1991, paperback, 1997).

Hill, Judith, 'Reputations: Nineteenth-century Monuments in Limerick', *History Ireland*, vol. 5, no. 4, Winter 1997, pp.44-48.

Hill, Judith, 'Davis Dukart and Christopher Colles: architects associated with the Custom House at Limerick', *Irish Architecture and Decorative Studies*, vol. II, 1999, pp.118-145.

Hill, Judith, 'New departure for Limerick', *Irish Arts Review*, 2003, pp.94-99.

Hodkinson, Brian, 'Summary report on the excavations at St Mary's Cathedral, Limerick, 1992', *North Munster Antiquarian Journal*, vol. 37, 1996, pp.37-64.

Hodkinson, Brian, 'Summary report on two sites in the Medieval town of Limerick', *North Munster Antiquarian Journal*, vol. 39, 1998-99, pp.13-77.

Hodkinson, Brian, 'Thom Cor Castle; a 14th Century Tower House in Limerick City?', *Journal of the Royal Society of Antiquaries of Ireland*, vol. 135, 2005, pp.119-129.

Hodkinson, Brian, 'St John's Gate and the Citadel in Irishtown, Limerick', *North Munster Antiquarian Journal*, vol. 46, 2006, pp.129-131.

Laffan, William, ed., *Painting Ireland; Topographical Views from Glin Castle* (Tralee, 2006).

Lee, David and Christine Gonzalez, eds, *Georgian Limerick 1714-1845*, vol. II (Limerick, 2000).

Lee, David, *James Pain Architect* (Limerick, 2005).

Logan, John, '"Dropped into this Kingdom from the clouds": The Irish career of Davis Dukart, architect and engineer, 1761-81', *Irish Architectural and Decorative Studies*, vol. X, 2007, pp.34-89.

O'Flaherty, Eamonn, *Irish Historic Towns Atlas, Limerick* (Dublin: to be published in 2009).

O'Keeffe, Peter and Tom Simington, *Irish Stone Bridges: History and Heritage* (Dublin, 1991).

Ó'Tuathaigh, Gearóid, Liam Irwin and Matthew Potter, eds, *Limerick: History and Society* (Dublin, to be published in 2008).

Potter, Matthew, *The Government and the People of Limerick: The History of Limerick Corporation/City Council 1197-2006* (Limerick, 2006).

Rothery, Seán, *A Field Guide to the Building of Ireland* (Dublin, 1997).

Rothery, Seán, *Ireland and the New Architecture* (Dublin, 1997).

Spellissy, Seán, *Limerick in old photographs* (Dublin, 2003).

Thomas, Avril, *The Walled Towns of Ireland*, vols 1 and 2 (Dublin, 1992).

Wiggins, Kenneth, *Anatomy of a Seige: King John's Castle, Limerick, 1642* (Wicklow, 2000).

Williams, Jeremy, *A Companion Guide to Architecture in Ireland, 1837-1921* (Dublin, 1994).

ATHLUNKARD BRIDGE
Corbally Road

Registration Numbers

The structures mentioned in the text of this Introduction are listed below. It is possible to find more information on each structure by accessing our survey on the Internet at: www.buildingsofireland.ie and searching by the Registration Number, structure name, or location. Please note that the majority of the structures included in this book are privately owned and not open to the public. However, ecclesiastical buildings such as churches, public buildings such as shops, hotels, public houses, banks and railway stations in use, are normally accessible. Courthouses and some other buildings have variable access. Structures are listed by page number.

08-09 King John's Castle,
King's Island
Not included in survey.

12-13 John's Gate,
Grounds of St John's Hospital
Reg. 21513067

14-16 St Mary's Cathedral, Nicholas
Street/Athlunkard Street
Reg. 21508014

17 Fanny's Castle, Mary Street
Not included in survey.

17 House, Curry's Lane
Reg. 21513035

17 King's Mills
Not included in survey.

17 Laxweir
Not included in survey.

17 Dominican Friary, Englishtown
Not included in survey.

18 Bastion, King John's Castle
Not included in survey.

18 The Exchange, Nicholas Street
Reg. 21513057

19 John's Gate,
Grounds St John's Hospital
Reg. 21513067

22-23 Dominican Chapel,
Fish Lane
Demolished.

22 Dutch Gable, rear of Johns'
Square
Not included in survey.

22 Gable, Broad Street
Not included in survey.

22-23 Bishop's Palace, Church Street
Reg. 21508003

22, 24 John's Square
Regs. 21513044-37,
21518036-40

25 The Exchange, Nicholas Street
Reg. 21513057

25 Gaelscoil, (former City
Courthouse), Bridge Street
Reg. 21513056

25 Blue Coat School,
Nicholas Street
Reg. 21508021

28 Lock Mills, Lock Quay
Reg. 21513049

28 Bank Place
Regs. 21513010-21513012

28-29 Assembly House,
Assembly Mall
Demolished.

30-31 The Hunt Museum, (former
Custom House), Rutland Street
Reg. 21513013

32 Williams Stores,
4 Patrick Street
Reg. 21513005

32 The Granary, Bank Place
Reg. 21513017

32-33 Lock Mills, Lock Quay
Reg. 21513049

36-37 68 O'Connell Street
Reg. 21517208

36-37 17-29 Mallow Street
Reg. 21517213-21517218;
21517305-21517311

37 Mews Building,
Catherine Street
Not included in survey.

37 Dovecot, Chamber of
Commerce, 96 O'Connell
Street
Reg. 21517045

38 Limerick Printmakers,
Robert Street
Reg. 21513021

38 The Round House,
High Street/Back Lane
Reg. 21518055

38-39 Bishop's Palace,
104 Henry Street
Reg. 21517022

38-39 Former Henry Hartstonge
House, 103 Henry Street
Reg. 21517021

40 11-24 Lower Hartstonge Street
21517086-21517097; 21517084
75-77 O'Connell Street
21517081-21517083

40-41 1-6 Hartstonge Street
Regs. 21517222-21517227

40 Conradh Na Gaeilge,
18 Thomas Street
Reg. 21518004

40 17-29 Mallow Street
Reg. 21517213-21517218;
21517305-21517311

40 6-12, 23-36,
28 Glentworth Street
Regs. 21517239-21517243;
21517268-21517272;
21517312-21517313

40 52-53 Catherine Street
Not included in survey.

42 Houses, O'Connell Street
Regs. 21517023-21517024;
21517027-21517028;
21517044-21517049;
21517059-21517067;
21517076; 21517078-
21517083; 21517202-
21517212; 21517229-
21517330; 21517333-
21517338; 21517252;
21517254-21517255;
21517258-21517261; 21517323

42 Houses, Cecil Street
21517030-21517038;
21517042; 21517085;
21517232; 21517262;
21517262-21517264;
21517321-21517322;
21517324; 21518010-21518011

42 4 The Crescent; 5 The
Crescent; 56 O'Connell Street;
57 O'Connell Street; 8 Mallow
Street
Regs. 21517198; 21517197;
21517235; 21517234;
21517249

42-43 4 The Crescent; 1 The
Crescent; 56 O'Connell Street;
70 O'Connell Street; 7 The
Crescent, 23 Mallow Street
Regs. 21517198; 21517201;
21517235; 21517206;
21517195; 21573311

42, 44 79 O'Connell Street;
72 O'Connell Street;
4 The Crescent;
Regs. 21517079; 21517204;
21517198

42, 45 23 Barrington Street;
14 Barrington Street;
71 O'Connell Street
Regs. 21517165; 21517174;
21517205

42, 45 6 The Crescent
Reg. 21517196

46 Michael Martins,
Augustinian Lane
Not included in survey.

46 Tom Collins, 34 Cecil Street
Reg. 21517264

46 P. Deegan, 34 Denmark Street
Reg. 21513019

46 Shop, High Street
Not included in survey.

47 Hamptons Estate Agents,
46 O'Connell Street
Reg. 21517259

47 3 Little Catherine Street
Reg. 21518003

48-49, 1-6 Pery Square
51 *Regs. 21517182-21517287*

50-51 House, Hartstonge Street
Reg. 21517189

52-54 Chamber of Commerce,
96 O'Connell Street
Reg. 21517045

55-56 Tippe Canoe/Carlton Coffee,
Shannon Street/Henry Street
Reg. 21512001

56 Limerick Printmakers,
4 Robert Street
Reg. 21513021

56   Newsoms, 20 Denmark Street
Reg. 21513025

53   The Mill Studio,
18 Upper William Street/
Old Windmill Lane
Reg. 21518029

53   Duggan Glass,
15 Roches Street
Reg. 21518007

53   Shannon Wholesale Electrical
Co. Ltd, 16 Roches Street/
Anne Street
Reg. 21518008

53   Estuary Wholesale Supply,
Roches Street
Reg. 21518021

56   Store, Thomas
Street/Augustinian Lane
Reg. 21518001

57   The Crescent
*Regs. 21517112-21517118,
21517191-21517201*

57   Spring Rice Memorial,
People's Park/Pery Square
Reg. 21517287

57   Fountain, People's Park
Reg. 21518018

57   Bandstand, People's Park
Reg. 21521087

58   Sarsfield Barracks,
Lord Edward Street
Regs. 21521082-21521083

59   Mid-West Business Institute
(former Commercial Buildings),
Patrick Street
Reg. 21513006

59   United Colours of Benetton
(former National Bank),
Sarsfield Street/Henry Street
Reg. 21512007

59   The Bank (former Provincial
Bank), 1 Mallow
Street/O'Connell Street
Reg. 21517228

59-60 Savings Bank, Glentworth
Street/Catherine Street
Reg. 21517293

61   St Saviour's Dominican
Church, Baker Place/
Dominick Street
Reg. 21518014

61   Quaker Meeting House,
Cecil Street
Reg. 21517265

61   McKerns Printers (former
Presbyterian Meeting House),
Glentworth Street
Reg. 21517292

61   Health Service Executive
Building (former Trinity
Church), 31-33 Catherine
Street
Reg. 21517294

62   St Michael's Church of Ireland
Church, Pery Square
Reg. 21517177

62-63 Leamy House (former Leamy's
Free School), Hartstonge Street
Reg. 21517190

62-63 Former Villiers Schools,
Henry Street
Reg. 21517019

64   Sarsfield Bridge (former
Wellesley Bridge), Sarsfield
Street/Ennis Road
Reg. 21512010

64   The Graving Dock, Dock
Road/James Casey Walk
Reg. 21517043

66-67 Former House of Industry,
Clancy's Strand
Reg. 21512018

66-67 St Camillus's Hospital (former
Limerick Union Workhouse),
Shelbourne Road
Reg. 21506001

68-69 St Joseph's Hospital (former
Limerick District Asylum),
Mulgrave Street
Reg. 21519002

68-69 Limerick Prison (former
County Gaol), Mulgrave Street
Reg. 21518047

68-69 City Hall (former City Gaol),
Crosbie Row
Reg. 21508013

68-69 County Gaol, Merchant's Quay
Demolished.

69   Limerick Senior College
(former County Infirmary),
Mulgrave Street
Reg. 21518045

69   Artillery Barracks, Mulgrave
Street/Newtownmahon
Reg. 21518033

69   County Courthouse,
Merchant's Quay
Reg. 21513060

69   The Potato Market,
Merchant's Quay
Reg. 21513061

70-71 Island Theatre Company
(former St Munchin's Church
of Ireland Church), Church
Street
Reg. 21508007

71   Villiers Almshouses,
Old Dominick Street
Reg. 21508009

72   Athlunkard Bridge,
Corbally Road
Reg. 21502002

72   Baal's Bridge,
Mary Street/Broad Street
Reg. 21513031

72-73 Thomond Bridge,
Castle Street/High Road
Reg. 21508001

72-73 Tollhouse, Verdant Place
Reg. 21508002

74   Barrington's Hospital,
George's Quay
Reg. 21513053

74   The Milk Market, Broad
Street/Cornmarket Street
Reg. 21513028

75   Laurel Hill,
South Circular Road
Not included in survey.

75   Ashbourne,
South Circular Road
Not included in survey.

75   Mary Immaculate College
(former Summerville House),
Summerville Avenue
Reg. 21520001

75   Ardscoil Rís
(former Shelbourne House),
North Circular Road
Reg. 21511015

75   Villier School (former Tivoli),
North Circular Road
Reg. 21515004

75   Bellevue, North Circular Road
Reg. 21511018

75   Sunville, North Circular Road
Reg. 21515001

75   Kilmoyle, North Circular Road
Reg. 21511009

75   Clarion Hotel (former Ardhu
House), Ennis Road
Reg. 21511001

75   Beechlawn,
North Circular Road
Reg. 21511019

76   Houses, O'Connell Avenue
*Regs. 21517154-21517157;
21521021-21521041;
21521044-21521045; 21521056*

76   Houses, South Circular Road
*Regs. 21521003-21521007;
21521047-21521053*

76-77 Houses, Ennis Road
*Regs. 21512033-21512035;
21512040-21512045;
21512048-21512051*

76, 78 Boru House, Mulgrave Street
Reg. 21519001

78   Workers' Cottages,
Lord Edward Street
Not included in survey.

78   Workers' Cottages,
Thomondgate
Not included in survey.

78   Workers' Cottages,
Englishtown
Not included in survey.

79   Colbert Railway Station,
Parnell Street
Reg. 21518019

80-81 Bord Gáis, Dock Road
Reg. 21517005

81   Bord Gáis Power Station,
O'Curry Street
Reg. 21517006

81   Golden Vale (former
Lansdowne Flax Mill),
North Circular Road
Reg. 21512053

81   Chimneystack (former
Lansdowne Flax Mill),
North Circular Road
Reg. 21512059

81   Prospect Hill Clothing Factory
(former Tait's Army Clothing
Factory), Lord Edward Street
Reg. 21521085

81   Sarsfield Barracks (former New
Barracks), Lord Edward Street
Reg. 21521082-21521083

82   Bannatyne Mills, Dock Road
Reg. 21516002

83   Model School,
O'Connell Avenue
Reg. 21521043

Acknowledgements

NIAH

Senior Architect William Cumming
Survey Controller Mildred Dunne
GIS/IT Deborah Lawlor
Additional NIAH Staff Ruth Derwin, Eugene Finnerty, Gareth John, Damian Murphy, Alan Murray, T.J. O'Meara, Barry O'Reilly, Jane Wales, Ann Kennedy and Emer Mulhall.

The NIAH gratefully acknowledges the assistance of the following in the preparation of the Limerick City Survey and Introduction:

Survey Fieldwork

Charles Duggan, Stephen Farrell and Gretta Doyle.

Introduction

Writer Judith Hill
Editors Mildred Dunne, Barry O'Reilly and William Cumming
Photographers Don Allen, Stephen Farrell and Donal Dunne
Designed by Bennis Design
Printed by Brunswick Press

The NIAH wishes to thank all of those who allowed access to their property for the purpose of the Architectural Inventory of Limerick City and subsequent photography.

The NIAH particularly wishes to acknowledge the generous assistance give by: Desmond FitzGerald, The Knight of Glin; William Laffan, Celie ORahilly, Brian Hodkinson, Edward Chandler, Liz and Mark Skehan, Dara McGrath, Donal Dunne, Frances Clarke, the staff of the Irish Architectural Archive, the staff of the National Photographic Archive and the National Library of Ireland; Tony Roche and the staff of the Photographic Unit of the Department of the Environment, Heritage and Local Government, Con Manning and Tom Condit and our archaeological colleagues in the Department of the Environment, Heritage and Local Government; Ken Bergin and Jean Turner, Special Collections Library, University of Limerick; Dr. John Logan, University of Limerick; Manuscripts Department, Trinity College Dublin; Early Printed Books, Trinity College Dublin; The British Library; National Monuments Record, English Heritage; Fiona Davern, the Hunt Museum; Tom Keogh and Larry Walsh, Limerick Museum; Gary MacMahon, Copper Reed Studio; Jill Fenton, Island Theatre Company; Siobhán O'Reilly, The Limerick City Gallery of Art; Limerick City Council; Limerick Civic Trust; McKerns Print and Design, Glentworth Street; Blom Aerofilms Limited, Somerset; Denis O'Kelly, Murrary O'Laoire Architects; Donough Cahill, Irish Georgian Society and Peter Holder, Irish Historical Picture Company.

Sources of Illustrations

The illustrations listed below are identified by their figure and/or page number:

Book front cover, figs. 26, 109 are the work of Donal Dunne; page 2, page 4 (bottom), figs. 2-3, 7-13, 16-17, 21, 29, 34, 38, 46, 51, 54, 57-58, 64, 69, 76, page 47 (top left, top right, bottom left), figs. 78, 80, 83, page 54 (left image); figs. 85, 87, 89, 90, 92, 95-97, 99, 101, 105, 106, 108, 110-113, 115-116, 118, 122-124, 132, 135-136, 137, 139-142, 146-148, page 94, figs. 152-158, 162-163, 165-173, 175-182, page 111, page 112, page 120 are the work of Don Allen; page 4 (top), fig. 14, page 21 (bottom), page 26 (bottom), figs. 45, 77, page 65, page 66 (both images), page 76, figs. 121, 125, 138, page 91 (bottom left), fig. 149 are the property of the National Library of Ireland and have been reproduced with the permission of the Council of Trustees of the National Library of Ireland; figs. 1, 42 are courtesy of the British Library; fig. 4 is used courtesy of Celie ORahilly; figs. 5, 44 are reproduced courtesy of Trinity College Dublin; figs. 6, 18-19, 22-25, 33, 41, 91, page 63 (bottom), fig. 103, page 68 (bottom left), fig. 119 are courtesy of Limerick City Museum; page 13 is courtesy of the Hunt Museum; page 15 (top left), figs. 15, fig. 28, 32, 37, 39-40, 50, 52-53, 56, 59-63, 65-68, page 47 (bottom right), 81-82, 84, 86, page 53 (top three and bottom left), page 54 (top right and bottom right), figs. 93-94, 102, 114, 117, 120, 126-131, 133-134, page 89 (top), figs. 150-151, 159-161, 174, page 115 are the work of Stephen Farrell; fig. 20 is courtesy of the Photographic Unit, Department of the Environment, Heritage and Local Government; page 20, fig. 30, page 26 (top), figs. 36, 104 are reproduced courtesy of the Leonard Collection, University of Limerick; page 21 (top), figs. 27, 31, page 30 (bottom), figs. 47-48, 70-75, 79, 81, page 52, page 53 (bottom right), figs. 100, 164 are used courtesy of Judith Hill; page 27, figs. 35, 98 are courtesy of The Knight of Glin; fig. 43 is courtesy of English Heritage; figs. 49, 55 are reproduced courtesy of the Irish Architectural Archive; fig. 77 is courtesy of Edward Chandler; fig. 88 is courtesy of the Irish Historical Picture Company; fig. 107 is courtesy of the Tom Keogh Collection; figs. 143-145 are courtesy of the Copper Reed Studio.

The NIAH has made every effort to source and acknowledge the owners of all of the archival illustrations included in this Introduction. The NIAH apologises for any omissions made, and would be happy to include such acknowledgements in future issues of this Introduction.

Please note that most of the structures included in the Architectural Inventory of Limerick City are privately owned and are therefore not open to the public.

ST ALPHONSUS LIGUORI
REDEMPTORIST CHURCH
South Circular Road